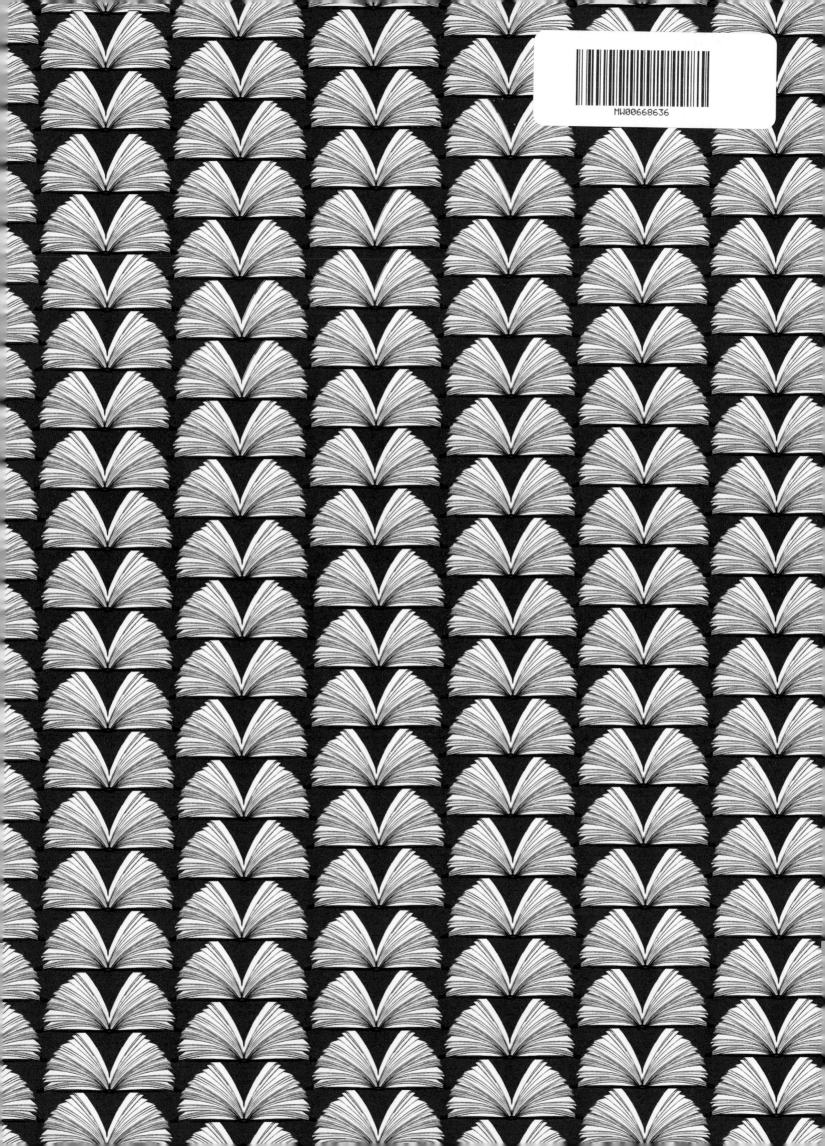

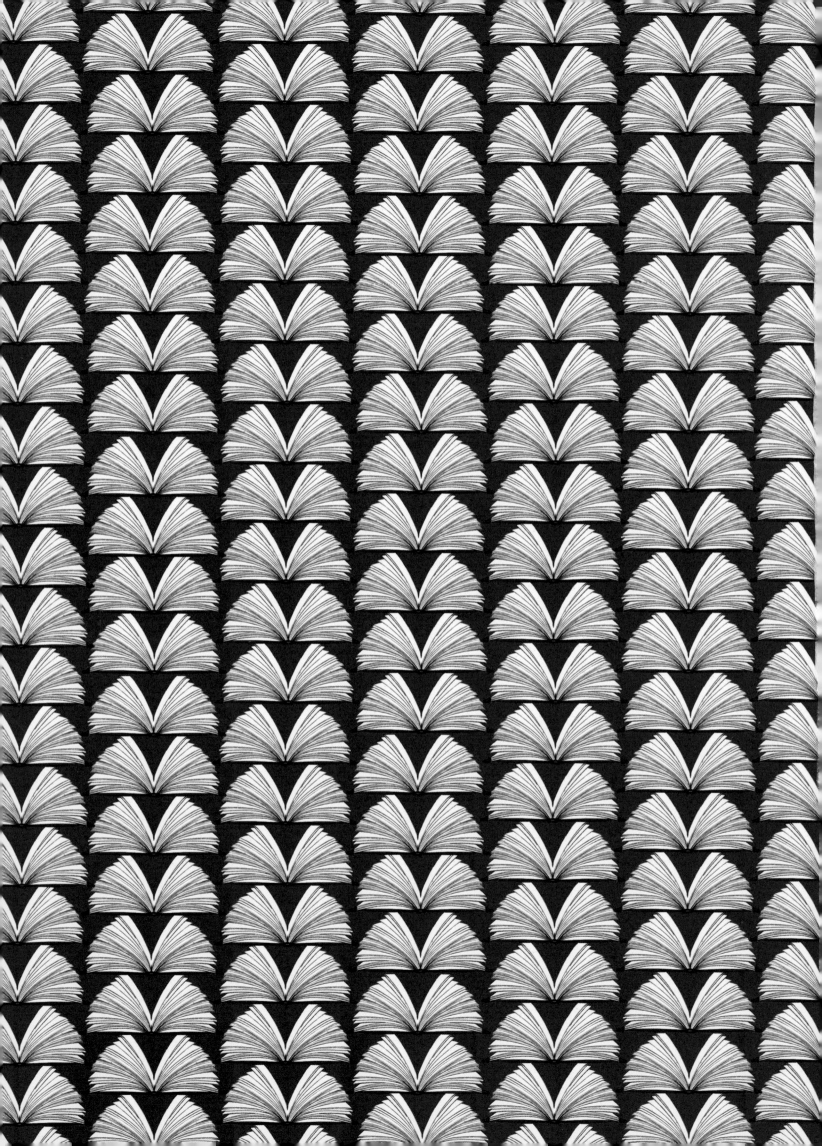

For the Love of Books

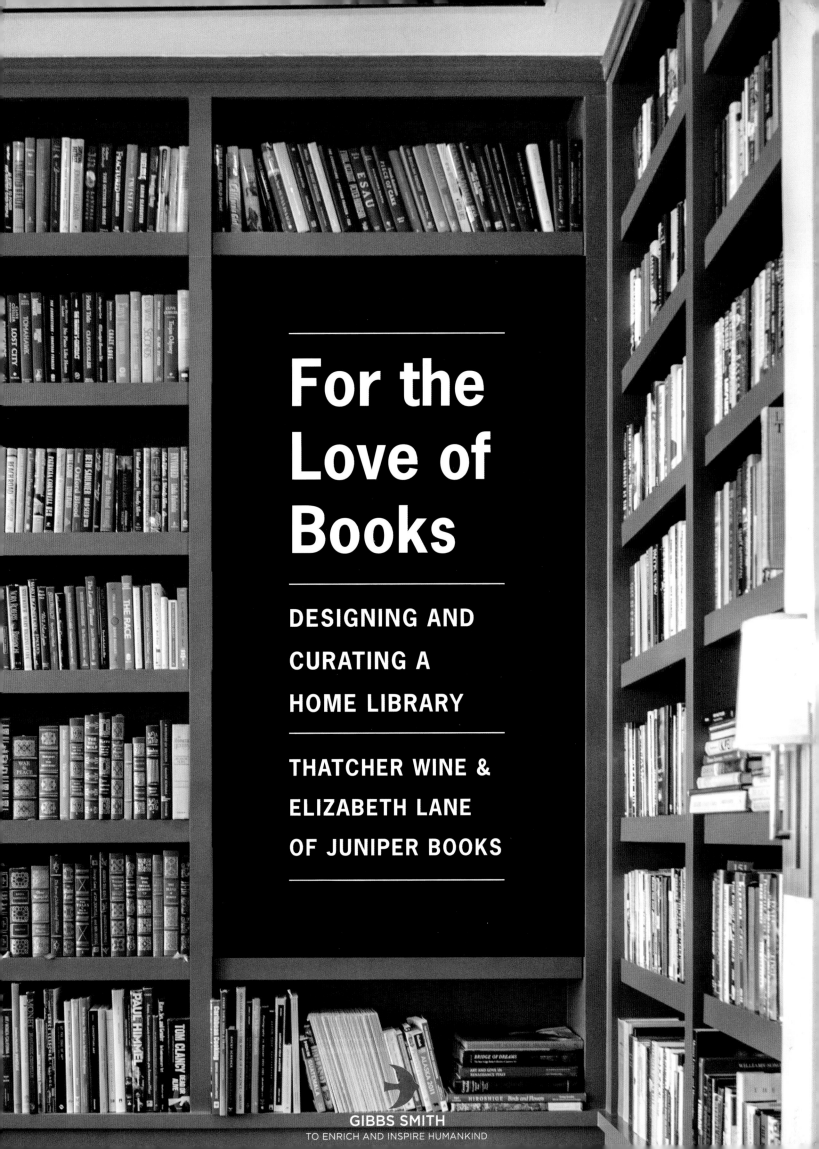

For the Love of Books

DESIGNING AND
CURATING A
HOME LIBRARY

THATCHER WINE &
ELIZABETH LANE
OF JUNIPER BOOKS

GIBBS SMITH
TO ENRICH AND INSPIRE HUMANKIND

First Edition
23 22 21 20 19   5 4 3 2 1

Interiors featured in the homes of:
Elizabeth Antonia: pages 116, 120 (left), 126, 130, 156
Christene Barberich: pages 31, 67, 113 (top right), 136
Helen Dealtry: pages 49, 51, 54 (bottom), 66, 200, 250
Jeanine Hays and Bryan Mason: pages 150 (top left),
153, 170
John Petersen/Riley Kinnane-Petersen: page 128
Claudia Wu: pages 40, 103, 108

Published by
Gibbs Smith
P.O. Box 667
Layton, Utah 84041

1.800.835.4993 orders
www.gibbs-smith.com

Jacket design by Jenny Carrow
Front cover photograph by Kylie Fitts
Interior design by Debbie Berne
Printed and bound in China

Gibbs Smith books are printed on either recycled, 100%
post-consumer waste, FSC-certified papers or on paper
produced from sustainable PEFC-certified forest/
controlled wood source. Learn more at www.pefc.org.

Library of Congress Cataloging-in-Publication Data:

Names: Wine, Thatcher, 1972- author. | Lane, Elizabeth
(Bookseller), author. | Juniper Books (Boulder, Colo.)
Title: For the love of books : designing and curating
a home library / Thatcher Wine & Elizabeth Lane of
Juniper Books.
Description: Layton, Utah : Gibbs Smith, [2019]
Identifiers: LCCN 2018060862 | ISBN 9781423652151
(hardcover)
Subjects: LCSH: Book collecting. | Private libraries. |
Books in interior decoration.
Classification: LCC Z987 .W497 2019 | DDC
002.075—dc23
LC record available at https://lccn.loc.gov/2018060862

For Cedar and Jasmine, Edie and Emily

Contents

"A room without books is like a body without a soul."

—Marcus Tullius Cicero

A Note to Our Readers

You don't have to be a voracious reader to love surrounding yourself with books or enjoy having books in your home. Books make us feel comfortable; they are sources of inspiration, information, and entertainment.

If you are holding this book in your hands, odds are you already love books. Most likely, we're not trying to convince you of a new hobby or interest. This book is more about identifying the meaning in it all—what all those books on your shelves say about you and what you can do to have them say a little more, more clearly.

The ideas and images in this book are shared to inspire a more enriching life through books—both reading them and decorating with them. Perhaps they encourage you to bring more books into your home or to highlight what you already have in a new way. If the pages unfold and allow you to dream of possibilities never considered with books, we will be thrilled.

In the fast-paced, digitally saturated, screen-overloaded era we live in, we believe that printed books are a refuge of space and time. It's OK to slow down and read; it's OK to fill your home and your shelves with printed books and to celebrate the comfort and meaning they provide in our lives. We believe it's something that we all crave whether we know it or not.

One final note before we get to the books. We believe that if you print something and it takes up physical space, it should be worth keeping forever. We hope that we've written and designed this book to be worthy of a space on your coffee table or bookshelves and that it becomes part of your story in the same way that your books are interwoven with who you are.

Mother
+
Elizabeth

Introduction

I've always loved books and being surrounded by books, but I didn't originally set out to become a bookseller or work in the book trade.

There were some early indications about my future career that I didn't think much of at the time. When I was eight, I took an old book to Sotheby's for a kids' appraisal day. It turned out not to be worth much, but I made the local TV news—my first press appearance! They referred to me as Wine Thatcher, not the last time my name would be mixed up.

I remember the day and the feeling I had when I finished reading Michael Ende's *The Neverending Story* and had to begrudgingly hand it back over the counter to the school librarian. Not only did I come to the end of the book that was not supposed to end, but I couldn't even keep my new favorite book on my shelves!

Selling books began as a hobby for me in the summer of 2001. The online customer service company I had started ran out of money that year and I needed to figure out what to do next. I soon found that I loved telling the story of the books I held in my hands—mostly old books, antiquarian tomes with previous owners' names and notes in the margins.

From day one, what intrigued me the most about books was the infinite potential for storytelling that didn't start or finish with the content on the pages. Authors have a backstory of their own and while they may write books, they generally don't sell them. It's up to others to tell the complete story about that specific book.

As I sold more books and got requests to build collections for clients, I started thinking of how a group of books together on the shelf could tell an even bigger story. A collection of books said a lot about what the books had in common. They also reflected the interest and personality of the person whose shelf they were on.

What I've realized over the past eighteen years is something that I think we all know—printed books are magic and they have unlimited potential to engage us. As we look at our shelves, we also sense that printed books have the ability to do all these things and more without even opening their covers. They tell a story whether their covers are open or shut, whether they are on the shelves or in our hands.

I invite you to explore the possibilities of storytelling with books around your home as we take you on a journey that will hopefully enrich your life.

Thatcher

Hemingway

Selected Letters 1917-1961

Islands in the Stream

Death in the Afternoon

A Farewell to Arms

The Sun Also Rises

THE HANDMAID'S TALE

ATWOOD

PART ONE

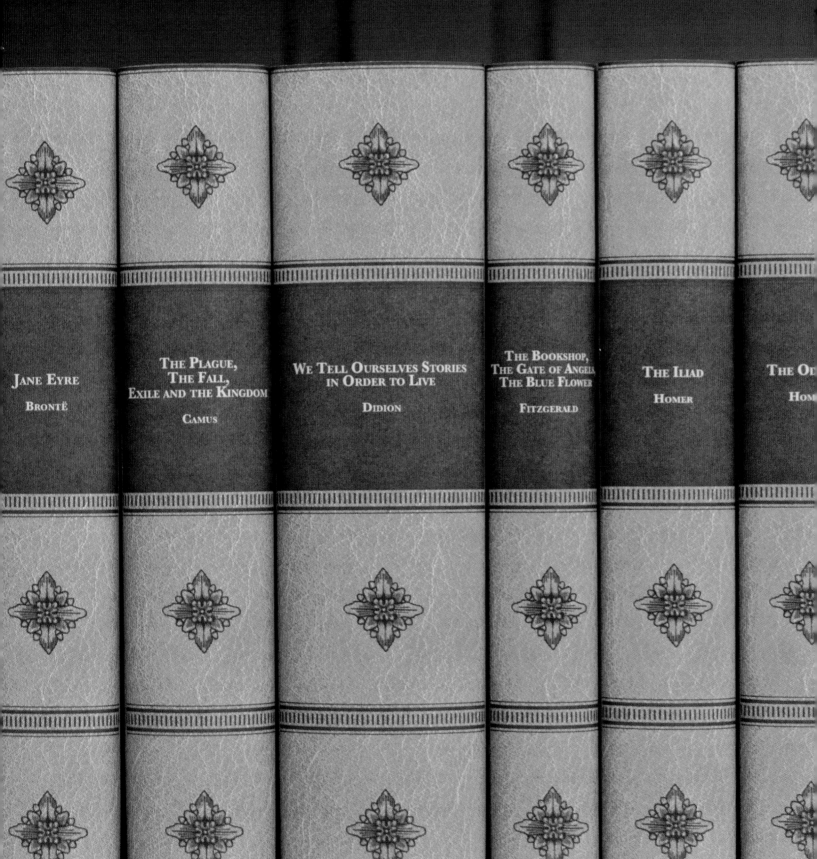

rezzo. Questo amore è secondo lo spirito: imperciocchè non ha quì luogo la carne. Io diffido assai di messtesso, e per questo vorrei, che mi lasciaffero vivere secondo questa inclinazione; chi non vede, che non è questo vivere secondo lo spirito? No ceramente, mia carissima Figlia; perchè quando io era ancora assai giovane, nè ancor avea spirito, Io già viveva così: ma quandunque, atteso il mio naturale io sia timido ed apprensivo, contuttociò io vogliassonarmi di vincere queste passioni naturali; e a poco a poco eseguir appunto ciò, che risguarda la Carica, che obbedienza, che il Signore da Dio, che quello chi non vede, che

The Books We Keep,
the Stories We Tell

"WE TELL OURSELVES stories in order to live," Joan Didion starts her first essay in *The White Album*[1] with this sentence, detailing our human instinct to make sense of the incomprehensible, to link life's naturally disparate scenes with a narrative thread. On instinct, we fill in the blanks to create stories and these stories then create our realities. Whether we know it or not, we are always telling stories.

We share these stories in every moment in myriad ways; it's human nature to do so. We live by these stories and extract our ways of being from them. We shape our experience through the lens of stories and often try to shape another's experience through that same lens.

For much of human history our stories were shared orally. Later, forms of writing appeared, followed by the creation of the alphabet, printing, and finally digitization and the internet. Words took flight on a global scale, bringing stories in increasingly efficient ways to a wider audience.

This timeless urge to share our stories has sparked the greatest technological innovations, like writing, the alphabet, the printing press, and the internet, as mentioned above.

Our stories have formed the foundation of civilizations, incited revolutions, and restored stability during times of unrest. Whether fiction or nonfiction, our history is indeed written in stories.

However, our storytelling does not begin and end with words on a page. The idea that a collection of books or a library can tell the story not only of civilizations, but of us as individuals, is a theme that we will come back to many times throughout this book.

For every printed book (or clay tablet, papyrus scroll, or hand-copied manuscript), the written word has proliferated from one person (the author) to many (the readers). The places where these works have been stored each contribute their own piece of the text's story, whether it is a government repository, a spiritual archive, a community library, or a home bookshelf.

The story of each place is unique. For example, a library that holds a first edition of *The Great Gatsby* has a different tale to tell than one that has the paperback edition circulated in high school classrooms. The location, how the book was acquired, and where the book is placed among other books and personal items all enhance our experience with F. Scott Fitzgerald's classic work. The story is not just his—it is ours.

"We tell ourselves stories in order to live. . . . We interpret what we see, select the most workable of the multiple choices. We live entirely . . . by the imposition of a narrative line upon disparate images, by the 'ideas' with which we have learned to freeze the shifting phantasmagoria—which is our actual experience."

—Joan Didion, *The White Album*

Across the River and into the Trees
The Sun Also Rises
The Short Stories
For Whom the Bell Tolls
Selected Letters 1917-1961
Islands in the Stream
Death in the Afternoon

steinbeck

THE WORKS OF WILLIAM FAULKNER

Ernest Hemingway

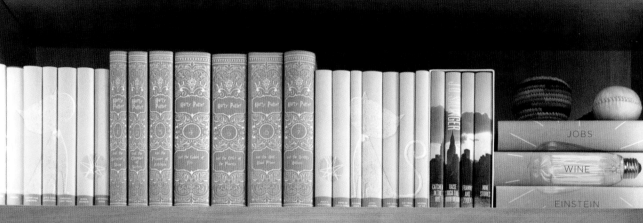

Harry Potter

JOBS

WINE

EINSTEIN

WILLIAMS-SONOMA

1,000 GLUTEN-FREE Recipes

gluten free

The Family Meal

Home cooking with Ferran Adrià

NOMA

René Redzepi

benu

corey lee

Sicily

THE ART OF FRENCH BAKING

BRICE MARDEN

JACKSON POLLOCK

ROBERT RAUSCHENBERG

JOSEPH BEUYS

CHUCK CLOSE

RICHARD ESTES

ANSELM KIEFER

ANDY WARHOL

DAVID SMITH

GEORGIA O'KEEFFE

FRANCIS BACON

SHERLOCK HOLMES

Sir Arthur Conan Doyle

John Rewald CÉZANNE

AMERICAN MONUMENT

THE CHRONOLOGY of AMERICAN LITERATURE

AREA 2

100 Graphic Designers

10 Curators

10 Design Classics

MORANDI KAREN WILKIN

HOLE

W&G

MARSDEN HARTLEY AND THE WEST

Dieter Rams: As Little Design as Possible

Sophie Lovell

Perfect Neutrals

STEPHANIE HOPPEN

LEONARDO DA VINCI

MICHELANGELO

RAPHAEL

Meyer

American Great Illustrators

Georgia O'Keeffe Museum

Marks of Excellence

FRITZ KAHN

DESIGN WRITING RESEARCH

TUFTE VISUAL EXPLANATIONS

Abrams

TASCHEN

When we add books—any printed books—to our homes and lives and make space for them, something almost alchemical happens. We combine the author and *their* story with who we are and *our* story. The combination of the author and their story plus us and our story is a new story, and it's completely original.

Like our DNA, the combination of books we keep cannot be replicated by anyone else. Even if others have the same book titles as us, their books have different meaning to them. By holding books in our hands for hours as we read them, we develop associations that last forever: where we were when we bought the books, who we were when we read the books, where we keep our books, and how we organize them.

The books we keep are so much more than the stories on their pages and the titles on their spines, they are reflections of our choices, our preferences, ourselves.

We make choices about whether to keep a copy of *Wuthering Heights* or a biography of Winston Churchill, to give away that book about dog breeds that Aunt Alice gave us, or whether to buy a first edition of a beloved classic. These are acts of conscious choice and also acts of creative expression.

When we decide to keep a book and make space for it on our shelves, it becomes more than just a book. It becomes a placeholder, a breadcrumb, an invitation that we can return to at any time. Perhaps to re-read it; or just to think about it for a moment as we pass by; or to respond to a

guest who notices it and says, "I didn't know you were interested in philosophy." Walk into a stranger's home anywhere in the world—want to know something about them or what to talk about over dinner? Simply look at their bookshelves.

When we merge our books with a partner's and perhaps add children to the house, our bookshelves and libraries take on new meaning, serving to tell the story not just of one life and where we have been, but that of the entire family and our future.

We could choose to keep other things on our shelves—and many times we do—but nothing tells the story of who we are, where we have been, and where we are going like our books.

The books we keep reveal a story that is never-ending, it can constantly be rewritten, edited, and have chapters added, simply by changing the books on the shelf. Whether the books are in our hands or on our shelves, their covers open or shut, they keep on telling stories. And so should we.

So long as there are words on a page they will tell a story. And so long as there are printed books on the shelf they will tell a story. The books we keep are the stories we tell.

A BRIEF HISTORY
OF THE BOOK

Today, we thankfully have few, if any, limits on the books we read. Seemingly limitless books are available to us with one click. Within a few hours or days, a printed book is in our possession and anyone can have a library of hundreds or thousands of books in their home at a reasonable cost.

However, it has not always been this way. The earliest books took the form of clay tablets, then papyrus scrolls, and later parchment. They were hand copied before the invention of the printing press in the 1400s. When books were collected and stored in one place, they were largely a tool for control in service of a localized and defined power—either mortal or divine or both.

In Asia, where printing technology began, this technology was used not only as a means to spread information, but as a spiritual exercise for the divine—such as copying religious materials to gain merit with the Buddha.

The finest example of this practice is found in the text *The Diamond Sutra,* the earliest surviving printed book. *The Diamond Sutra* is a compilation of Buddhist teachings block-printed on seven sheets of paper and glued together into a scroll sixteen feet long. A colophon at the end of the document states its purpose—that Wang Jie had the scroll "reverently made for universal distribution . . . on behalf of his two parents" on May 11, 868.[2] *The Diamond Sutra* is a certain triumph of this earliest printing technology.

Along similar lines, in 1900, a chamber within a cave was discovered that had been sealed up more than one thousand years ago. Located outside of the town of Dunhuang, at the Gobi Desert's border in western China, the chamber contained more than five hundred cubic feet of collected manuscripts. Now referred to as the Dunhuang Library, the texts within remained inaccessible for more than nine hundred years.[3]

What was the intent behind sealing the chamber? Were these manuscripts trapped in the cave as an offering to a deity? It's very likely. In the early Middle Ages, Dunhuang flourished as a site of government and as a popular center for Buddhist worship. Pilgrims traveled far to visit their cave shrines—hundreds of lavishly decorated caverns carved into the cliff. It is likely then, similar to *The Diamond Sutra,* that the texts in the Dunhuang Library were collected as a divine spiritual exercise, an offering to and acknowledgment of the power of the divine.

The collection of manuscripts in the cave tells a story, though its precise meaning is mysterious to us a millennium after the collection's creation and placement. What is clear, however, is that a collection of manuscripts tells a different story than a single manuscript. For the most part, one manuscript would tell the story revealed on its pages. A collection of manuscripts, on the other hand, has the potential to reveal truths about the community and its power structure, their religious practices, and their communication methods.

Standing in contrast to Dunhuang is the Library of Alexandria, recognized as the earliest known library. King Ptolemy I Soter commissioned Demetrius of Phaleron to execute his plan in the third century BCE with the following vision: To create the world's greatest library in service to the study of the natural world and the heavens above,[4] housed within the *Mouseion*—the sacred temple of the Ptolemies dedicated to the Muses.

The library sought to store *every* piece of writing that passed through the port, and toward this aim, leadership got creative. As one story describes,

> Ptolemy III Euergetes, or "Benefactor," the third of his line to take the Alexandrian throne, was determined to be as beneficent as possible to the Mouseion's library, no matter the cost. Having borrowed a number of classic works from Athens in exchange for a hefty deposit—fifteen talents of silver, totaling around more than 850 pounds in weight—he had the Mouseion's scribes copy the originals before

sending the new versions back to the shocked Athenians. . . . The Athenians kept the silver, and the Mouseion kept the books."[5]

This story shows clear execution of the belief that knowledge is power—the civilization that holds the texts (the knowledge), holds the power. Furthermore, power can be expanded by developing new methods (and larger places) to store knowledge for future applications by the forces in control (government).

The story of Alexandria is one that fascinates us to this day. The exact date of the destruction of the library and its priceless contents (estimates range from 40,000 to 400,000 manuscripts) is unknown. But we do know this: the Library of Alexandria had a reputation throughout the ancient world as a center of knowledge and learning, and this was a brand new story for the time.

Today we have libraries and universities circling the globe, they occasionally compete for the same rare books and papers for their archives. They also try to outdo each other in the quantity of their books and the quality of their architecture. The Library of Alexandria ushered in the era of the library as a source of power and influence that continues to this day.

In the fifteenth century (around 1450 CE), Johannes Gutenberg invented the functional printing press, making what was once a laborious handmade task delegated to scribes into a mechanized revolution. By the century's close, printing had spread to no less than 236 countries in Europe, with more than twenty million books produced. In 1455, all of Europe's printed books could have been carried in a single wagon. Fifty years later, the number of book titles printed ran into tens of thousands, the total quantity of books printed was in the millions.[6]

With mass printing that Gutenberg's printing press allowed, it became possible for the everyday person to more readily acquire books, making the elite luxury of a personal library an increasingly democratic possibility. As books became more accessible, ideas circulated with greater ease. With knowledge, the locus of power became dispersed, causing a shift that, as expected, created discomfort.

With books flooding the market in the late fifteenth and early sixteenth centuries, those in this new printing profession were regarded with deep suspicion as it was hard to reconcile the new technology with the deep-seeded belief that books were elite and rare in their very nature. What could books in quantities of the hundreds and thousands mean? A dangerous

political agenda? A supernatural act? Rumor holds that when Johann Fust, Gutenberg's ex-partner, went to Paris with cases full of books to sell, he was forced to flee, accused of being sent to do the devil's work.[7]

The story of printed books and the power they give individuals to tell their own story through the books they keep really starts with Gutenberg and his invention. In the ensuing decades, books started to flow into people's homes and with them flowed the power of storytelling. There was now unlimited potential to read something new and then become someone new.

The Resilience of the Printed Book in the Digital Era

THE EARLY 2000s witnessed the rise of e-books, smart-phones, and tablets. With the advent of the e-reader in the twenty-first century people felt a new sense of freedom and excitement. This new technology seemed to solve countless problems. We no longer needed to lug around heavy books for travel or choose just one book to bring, limiting our choices. We were free to impulsively purchase whatever title crossed our path, no discernment necessary. If we noticed someone reading a book on the subway, with a click it could be ours too.

So we found ourselves, as the first decade of the new millennium came to a close, with the sales of printed books declining and e-books soaring. It seemed that the long, successful run of Gutenberg's invention might be nearing the end of its useful life. From 2008 to 2012, e-book sales were rising quickly and were projected to surpass print book sales by 2017.

The idea of holding a stack of paper with words printed on it seemed quaint in an era when you can get the same words from "the cloud" whenever and wherever you want. Why carry around heavy books when you can load thousands of titles onto your device with one touch, buying books as quickly as it takes to load a web page?

As adoption of the new technology grew and readers developed new routines for discovering, purchasing, and consuming books, many changes flowed through our culture. Bookstores closed en masse, libraries were redesigned to accommodate more technology and fewer books, and many publishers scaled back their releases and print runs.

At the same time, lovers of the printed book were experiencing a certain sense of longing. The loss of the tactile connection with the book was certainly felt—the feel of the pages, the weight of the book in your hands, the smell of the paper—all essential to one's experience and relationship with the story.

Alongside the loss of this essential physicality, there was a loss that was more subtle and less tangible—that sense of connection between the story, time, and place—each informed by where we were when we bought the book, who we were when we read it, and the ways that we were reintroduced every time we looked at or pulled a book from the shelf. There is an intrinsic relationship between story and memory that entwines and interacts with the narrative as the senses engage.

MEDIA   DRILLING DOWN

Falling Sales for the Printed Word

By TEDDY WAYNE   APRIL 18, 2010

BOOKS

Curling Up With Hybrid Books, Videos Included

By MOTOKO RICH   SEPT. 30, 2009

TECHNOLOGY

E-Book Fans Keep Format in Spotlight

By BRAD STONE   OCT. 20, 2009

Pogue's Posts
The Latest in Technology From David Pogue

Some E-Books Are More Equal Than Others
JULY 17, 2009 12:57 PM

WORLD BUSINESS

Book Publishers Take Leaps Into Digital

By ERIC PFANNER   NOV. 9, 2008

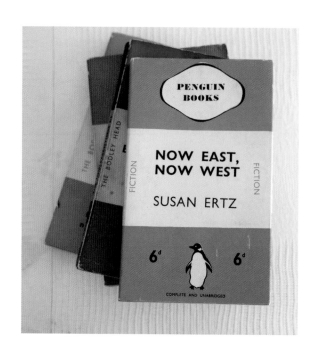

In 2008, Juniper Books had a major shift as Thatcher moved the business out of his basement and into a warehouse and studio space in Boulder, Colorado. From 2001 to 2008, the business had operated out of various basements, garages, and storage units. If the world was moving to e-books that took up no physical space, why was Juniper Books moving to a bigger commercial location with high ceilings and the capacity to do much more shipping and receiving than it had before?

Thatcher fielded numerous questions like this from his friends and family (and from the bank!). Was this the right time for business expansion? His friends in the technology business, where he had spent the first part of his career, thought he was crazy to be doubling down on analog. Who was buying or reading printed books anymore?

Architects and interior designers were now frequently designing houses entirely without bookshelves, believing that space for printed books was no longer needed. Clients wanted places to hang their flat screen TVs and they wanted shelves lined with electrical outlets to plug in their web-enabled photo frames, tablets, e-readers, and phones.

In resort communities like Beaver Creek, Colorado, designers told Thatcher that books looked "too small" in their large-scale homes. They wanted massive elk chandeliers and furniture made out of giant logs. Books looked out of place. Moreover, clients no longer traveled to their vacation homes with books in hand. They came with e-readers.

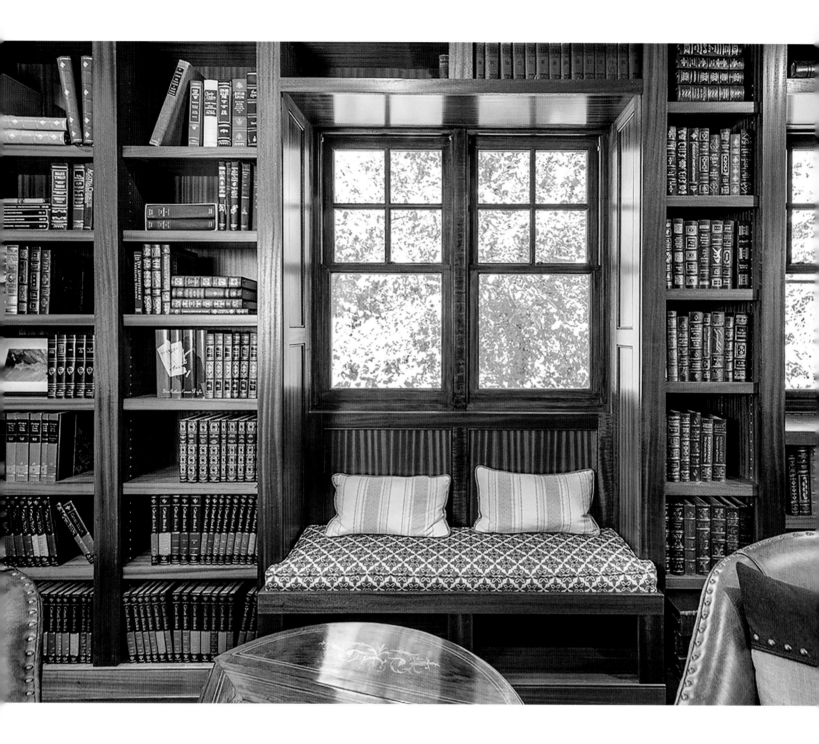

Yet, in the midst of the e-reader sensation, Thatcher sensed that true lovers of the printed book were becoming more dedicated than ever, and if he was hearing from even a few clients with nostalgia for print, then there must certainly be more out there. Thatcher also noticed that a certain demographic was approaching him with more frequency—clients in their fifties and sixties who had dreamed of building a library and retiring with free time to read their books. For these readers, a room of their own filled with printed books was a dream fulfilled.

As they reached this transition point in their lives, with empty nests and retirement within view, they envisioned a life filled with books, with reading. They could now read the classics that they didn't have time

to read while in the weeds, building their careers and raising their families.

Thatcher's clients shared with him time and again that they didn't work their whole lives—saving money, building their dream house, and their dream bookshelves—to reach this point and find out that printed books had become extinct, vanished like the dinosaurs. They wanted to fill their shelves with books while they still had time to enjoy them.

In the battle between printed books and e-books, Thatcher realized that printed books would always be loved and cherished by those who appreciated holding books in their hands and seeing them on

their shelves. The rise of the e-reader did not signal the demise of the printed book, rather it stimulated a newfound appreciation for a five-centuries-old technology that perhaps we had come to take for granted.

It was at this time, while at the crossroads contemplating the future of print in our culture and society, that Thatcher came to better understand the role that books play in the lives of individuals. While e-books are entertaining and convenient, they cannot replace all of the functions that printed books provide.

Juniper Books was not just selling books; it was helping clients understand and make sense of their lives, offering the opportunity to reclaim some space and time for themselves amid all the demands of modern society. Books are so much more than the plotlines mapped out on the pages, they are a way to understand the essence of who we are and then present that vision to the world on our shelves and in our homes.

With respect to space and time, books are like a wall of resistance against a world that demands everything we have to give.

Reading a book allows you to travel through space and time to other places, to see the world from other perspectives, and walk in another's shoes for a bit. Stories create possibilities for our limited vantages to be cracked open, affording new views and different experiences.

Reading forces us to slow down. In the fast-paced world we live, time is accelerating and we feel we have less of it. Our focus shifts second by second. We flip through our friends' updates on social media quickly to get the story. We get impatient when a song or a

The Resilience of the Printed Book in the Digital Era 37

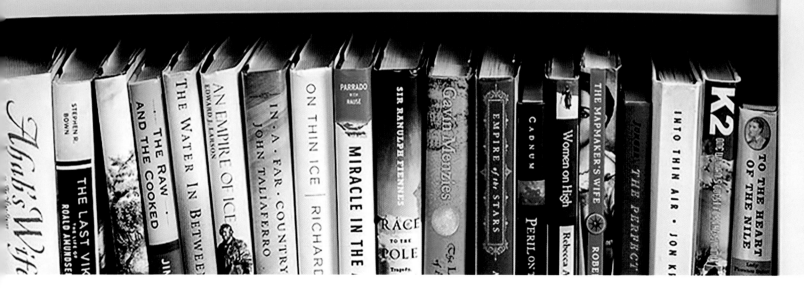

Part One

movie takes too long to download. We read on our devices, take a pause and check our email, check our texts. Our concentration is spent in bursts and the sense of chaos builds.

And we *are* in a time of chaos. Each one of us can feel it. The pressure and the speed often feel relentless.

Who has time to read a book? That takes hours.

Who has time to write a book? That takes years.

And yet an author spent years writing every one of the books on our shelves.

We can feel the sense of time that a collection of books represents whether we know it consciously or not. We could look at our books and feel overwhelmed.

A sense of frustration with ourselves and our lives might creep in if we believe we don't have time to read any or all of our books.

But mostly we've found that books bring a sense of peace, calm, and quiet to a home. We know at some level that time spent with a book is *exactly* what we need.

When we look up from our phones at our bookshelves, we're reminded that we once had the time to spend ten or twenty hours with every one of those books. We know that before life became impossibly busy, we had more time to spend reading what we wanted to read. Perhaps then our books become a placeholder for the time we wish we had and hope we might have again one day.

Perhaps just a short time ago, reading a book was a part of your natural rhythm, an inclination to find the quiet within the chaos. When you had a few minutes to spare, you turned to a book. We yearn for this core sense of peace because we viscerally recognize it. And we have the freedom to claim it, to lean into the quiet and pick up a book. To claim this—to slow down and settle in with a story—this becomes a radical act of self-care. Reading *is* self-care.

As human beings living in a digital age, time-starved and rushing around, printed books are reminders of the time we once had, the time we want to have, and the time we hope to have. Printed books quell the chaos. Printed books make us feel comfortable and make us feel like everything is going to be OK.

EXERCISE

....

Think about one of your favorite printed books.

What comes to mind when you think about that book? Is it the plot? A character? Or is it something about the book's relationship to you? If you thought of your favorite Jane Austen or Ernest Hemingway novel, perhaps what came to mind was a feeling of holding the book in your hands, a sense of where on the pages a favorite scene or passage was printed, or a memory of whom you were dating at the time.

Now compare this to e-books. If you have read an e-book recently, think of your favorite book or just one that you consumed on your device via the cloud. It's a little different. Do you recall where you were when you read that book? How the device felt in your hands as you scrolled through the "pages"? Do you picture where in your list of downloads that book is? Maybe it's after the Malcolm Gladwell and before that scandalous romance novel you downloaded while on vacation—the one that you are relieved lives anonymously in the cloud rather than in physical form.

THE INVENTION OF
THE PAPERBACK

The iPhone hit the market in 2006. Steve Jobs introduced a device that was big enough to display "detailed, legible graphics, but small enough to fit comfortably in the hand and pocket." This device became the world's best-selling smartphone, changing the way we as a culture interact with our "devices" and, more significantly, with each other.

Seventy-five years ago, in a narrative that seems to foreshadow the dawn of the smartphone and e-reader, two innovators—Allen Lane in England and Robert de Graff in America—had a similar epiphany: they could change the reading habits of an entire culture just by making books smaller and more disposable, simultaneously changing the way we read *and* the way we perceive books.

In the 1930s, it was difficult for ordinary Americans to get their hands on good books. The country had only five hundred bookstores nationwide (in contrast there are approximately 2,200 independent bookstores today, not counting online retailers like Amazon), all clustered in the biggest twelve cities. There was also a significant monetary barrier as hardcovers cost $2.50 (equivalent to about $45 today). In response to this barrier to access, Allen Lane founded Penguin Books and Robert de Graff founded Pocket Books, bringing their idea of smaller, cheaper books to market.

This wasn't the first time books were covered in paper. In a sense, "paperbacks" are almost as old as moveable type. Historians trace the first paperback books to Aldus Manutius, a Venetian printer and publisher. At the start of the twentieth century, the French publishing houses primarily published in paperback (the first edition of James Joyce's *Ulysses,* published in Paris in 1922, is a paperback) and dime novels, or "penny dreadfuls"—lurid romances that were considered trashy by respectable houses, were sold in Britain before Penguin Books. Allen Lane's idea, though, was a bit different.

According to Penguin lore, Lane's *eureka* moment happened as follows:

> He just wanted a decent book to read. . . . Not too much to ask is it? It was
> in 1935 that Allen Lane, Managing Director of Bodley Head Publishers, stood
> on a platform at Exeter railway station looking for something good to read on
> his journey back to London. His choice was limited to popular magazines and

poor-quality paperbacks—the same choice faced every day by the vast majority of readers, few of whom could afford hardbacks. . . . Lane's disappointment and subsequent anger at the range of books generally available led him to found a company—and change the world . . . the quality paperback had arrived.[1]

Lane knew that if he provided intelligent books for a low price, the reading community would grow profoundly. Supply the books and the readers will follow. And so, in the summer of 1935, Lane launched Penguin Books with ten titles, including his friend Ms. Christie's novel *The Mysterious Affair at Styles.*

Robert de Graff, perhaps believing even more than Lane in the democratization of literature, launched Pocket Books in May 1939. With his prototype, a pocket-sized book measuring four-by-six inches and priced at a quarter, de Graff further pushed the needle in the book market by making books more

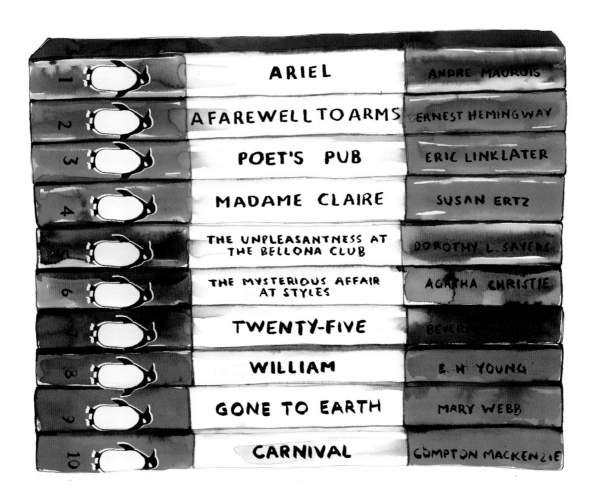

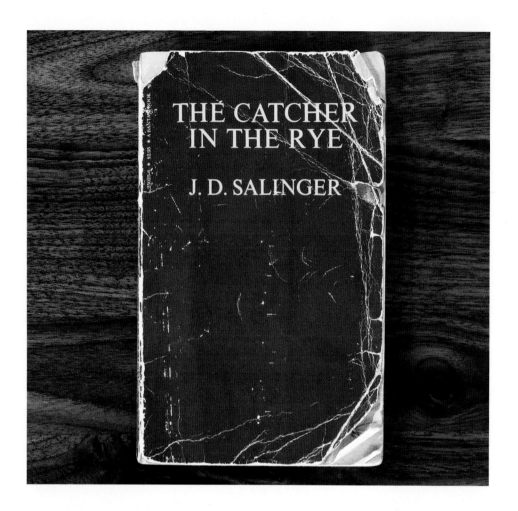

accessible with respect to size and price, exploding the potential on not only *who* would read, but *where* they would read.

As if overnight, it seemed that the public had a book in hand, similar to how we check our email or update our social media, our browsing no longer constrained by the cumbersome laptop. In continued contrast to Lane, de Graff wasn't concerned with the quality of literature. Instead he focused on mysteries and romances, the racier the better. Disrupting the book industry even further, de Graff worked with magazine distributors to place his books beyond the bookstore into grocery stores, drugstores, and airports. Within two years he'd sold seventeen million copies.[2]

The impact of the paperback was twofold. With their vast popularity, these little, inexpensive books put pressure on the hardcover publishing houses, which in turn put pressure on the legal regulation of print. There wasn't much regulation on books for paperback release, and so the more salacious story was often preferred. This resulted in a wider range of stories

that would be considered fit to print in both hardcover and paperback usher-
ing in a culture shift. The stories published in 1945 were vastly different than
those published just twenty years later. As Louis Menand reflects in *The New
Yorker,* without pulp paperbacks, there may not have been a Philip Roth or an
Erica Jong.[3]

One story about Thatcher's beloved maroon-covered copy of *The Catcher
in the Rye* fits well into this discussion. For the early paperback covers, the
cover designs tended to go after readers in the same way movie posters did
at the time, playing up the more risqué features, even if they were wholly
tangential to the storyline. When *The Catcher in the Rye* was published in
hardcover by Little, Brown, in 1951, sales were solid, but it was not the hit it
would become. For the paperback treatment, Salinger did not want his book
to have the typical pulp cover. Yet, in spite of Salinger's request, the Signet
edition came out in 1953 with the cover illustrated by "the Rembrandt of
Pulp," James Avati. Avati's cover shows Holden Caulfield standing outside
what appears to be a Times Square strip club, the front cover blurb stating,
"This unusual book may shock you, will make you laugh, and may break
your heart—but you will never forget it!"[4] He clearly gave the public what
they wanted. By 1954, the paperback had sold 1.25 million copies. Even so,
Salinger was furious. When the paperback rights to *The Catcher in the Rye*
became available again and Bantam Books won the deal, Salinger designed
the all-text maroon cover himself, and also the simple geometric designs that
characterize his later novels.[5]

Books in Our Homes— How Did They Get There?

WHERE DO BOOKS COME FROM?

On the one hand, that's a simple question—they come from the mind of an author. They pass through the hands of an editor. A company publishes the book or at least provides a self-publishing service. A bookstore or online store then sells copies of the book to individuals who take the book home to read.

Books go from the mind of one person to the hands and minds of many readers. There is generally one story that the book tells and that story is repeated many times over as the book is read around the world, talked about in book groups, online reviews, and bookstores.

On the other hand, our bookshelves at home hold their own collection of stories. The murder mysteries, espionage thrillers, love stories—each one is a facet of the big story. Our shelves are not just the stories contained within the books but the stories of how those books came to be on our shelves.

These days many people buy books on Amazon.com, while others patronize local bookstores for a more personal experience. There are countless ways for a book to wind up on our shelves including from library sales, thrift shops, or specialty retailers like Anthropologie. Each of us has probably received books as gifts, or maybe borrowed one from the library and never returned it!

Do we still have the books that our parents gave us or that our grandparents had? Books we bought for school, and then kept? Books we picked up in an airport, or while traveling and supporting a local bookstore?

What about those select books our friends or romantic interests gave us to make a point. "Read page thirteen and tell me that's not us!" Where do those fit in?

Books that we bought because we wanted to read something *in that moment,* to be entertained.

Books we bought because we wanted to own those specific words on our shelves. That *exact* copy. Possession!

Perhaps you have a collection that didn't seem complete without all the books by John Steinbeck or all the books about Paul

Cézanne. Or all the books mentioned in *1,000 Books to Read Before You Die* (a lot of books!).

The point is that some books magically appear in our lives, like the ones given to us as children. Others are more intentional. They are "collected."

Almost everyone has a book collection whether they realize it or not. The books you read in school, the books you've been given by friends, the books you inherited from your parents or grandparents. There is a story in all of them. You can choose to tell this story in your present home, or to part ways with these books and tell a different story.

For those who have embarked on the journey to build their own book collection or a dream library with considered choices, there is a sincere intentionality to the process. There are also unlimited options that can feel overwhelming.

No matter how books enter our lives, we have a choice within any moment to decide what to do with them. We live in the material world, in buildings and houses. In most cases, we cannot keep unlimited amounts of stuff. We have to decide what is important to us and then decide where it goes.

Books are unlike other household objects in that one can have a "collection of books" without being a "book collector." There are very few objects that have so much versatility, that can be acquired at so little relative cost, and that function as decoration when not being used for entertainment or intellectual engagement.

The artwork on your walls serves as decoration, its purpose for visual enjoyment. You interact with your paintings by looking at them, you don't *also* take the canvases down and paint on them as a hobby.

On the other hand, the cookware in your kitchen is for cooking and not for decoration. Those pretty copper pots are one exception of course, but generally you do not just look at your cookware, you use it to make something.

Books play so many roles in our homes and our lives. We can read them and be entertained and learn something. We can keep them on the shelves and smile when we look at them, reminded of the tales within and the story they tell of who we are.

We can show them off to houseguests without reading from their pages—"I bought this copy in Paris while in college," or "This is a first edition I picked up at the town library sale."

There is nothing in our homes quite like a book. Wouldn't it be great if we could keep unlimited amounts of them? Books in every room, piled high, yet organized in such a

way that we knew where that exact title was, exactly when we wanted it.

Sadly the dream of infinite books is just a dream. Our space is limited and we can only keep so many books. That constraint forces choices. What if these choices and the decision-making that comes with them could be seen as a path to personal growth and understanding? We believe it is exactly that.

Just as the books we keep tell the story of who we are, the books we do *not* keep must be let go with an open heart and open mind. Letting a book go is an equally essential part of our ever unfolding story. We have to ask ourselves honestly, *why do I have this book?*

EXERCISE

....

To begin the process of letting go, let's
ask ourselves a few questions.

Are all of my books presently meaningful to me or is it time for some of them to go?

Do they reflect a past interest that is no longer "me"?

Do they hold secrets and sentimental attachments I still need to keep? For example the love poem inside the back cover of my college edition of Rilke.

Do I love the story within the book or this edition of the book? Is it time to upgrade my ratty paperback to a beautiful leather-bound edition?

Am I keeping this book because it's too hard to sell or donate?

A Book,
a Collection,
or a Library?

WE ALL KNOW what a book is, but how do you define a "collection" or a "library"? For us, there isn't an exact definition as books are personal to each individual and household. A collection may be two books, or it could be two thousand—what brings them together into a coherent collection is that they have a central theme.

A library could constitute perhaps one hundred books or thousands. Generally what unites a library is that all the books are in one place and a library can include a number of different collections within it. As we proceed through the next few chapters, we will discuss how you can have books for different purposes around your home, some combining to create collections, and even a library.

You can have a single book that doesn't go with the others. For Thatcher, a good example might be his grand-mother's *The Settlement Cook Book* or his grandfather's Hebrew prayer books.

Part One

They are sentimental books that represent a connection to the beloved grandparents who helped raise him. Does he read the books? Not really, but having them reminds him of his love for his family and their love for their books.

The subtitle of *The Settlement Cook Book—The Way to a Man's Heart*—is sexist and outdated. Thatcher loves to cook and his father was a celebrated chef; they both find the subtitle amusing and so keeping the book also becomes a reminder of generational and societal change.

You can have a collection of books that is not a library. Maybe it's your college textbooks, your deep dive into Eastern religion, or perhaps your collection of crafting books. A lot of people have lots of collections on a variety of topics. Over time, as our interests change, our books don't always represent what we are interested in in the here and now, or they don't do so proportionately to our interest level.

Elizabeth collects paperbacks that feature covers designed by Edward Gorey—not for the stories inside, purely for the covers.

Part One

You can buy a book for its cover and build an entire collection of books. Those aren't the only books in her house—it's just one of her collections and it makes traveling really fun when she finds a new Edward Gorey edition to bring back home. Owning a book for its cover, its illustrator, or whomever gave you the book is just as valid a reason to own a book as the words on the pages.

Thatcher has a collection about Colorado—approximately forty books. He doesn't have a library of books on Colorado, there isn't enough room on the shelves. However, he does have a library of a few hundred books that includes a variety of collections comprised of books about Dartmouth College (where he went to school) and the complete works of Kurt Vonnegut (one of his favorite authors). At the time of writing this book, he was thinking about selling his collection of books on Navajo rugs in order to free up some space.

The idea of a library of books conveys something much larger than a collection of books. You can fit a collection on a shelf or on a few shelves. A home library is typically at least one

Part One

room with bookshelves on multiple walls, but of course this criteria is fluid. A library can take many sizes, shapes, and forms.

A library lives on its own, whether it serves an entire community or one person. A library has its own unique identity, an element of "otherness" that is bigger and broader than a collection of books that carry a single theme, such as an author, a subject, or a style.

To illustrate how collections can be consolidated and highlighted within a library, a recent project in Texas is a good example. The client engaged Juniper Books to help them curate a two-story library in their new home. They wanted us to assist them in organizing the books they currently had while also elevating their current collection with additional books curated by us. The clients had approximately two hundred books that were important to them, and had room for about two thousand more books.

When Thatcher went to the home, he first set about getting a feel for the books they had on the shelves. In one corner of the room was an old family Bible. Scattered throughout the room were various prayer books, books about religion and spirituality, and books about religious leaders. Thatcher brought all the religion and spirituality books closer to the family Bible, then placed prayer books, hymnals, and other family heirlooms in adjacent spaces.

Faith was important to the family and so after the books were reorganized, that fact was presented much more clearly to anyone who saw their shelves. Their "collection" of religion and spirituality books now was highlighted within their "library" in a way that was commensurate with its importance to them.

anger WISDOM FOR COOLING
THE FLAMES

OXFORD

Perrault: The Complete Fairy Tales

RISING STRONG   BRENÉ BROWN PhD.
LMSW

ROME   Robert Hughes   KNOPF

SWEETBITTER   STEPHANIE DANLER

The Glass Menagerie   NDP874

LEAN IN   SHERYL SANDBERG

Random Family   SCRIBNER

Steve Jobs by Walter Isaacson

THE BOOK OF General Ignorance   John Lloyd & John Mitchinson

Tina Fey   Bossypants

Signet Classic   THE MYSTERIOUS STRANGER
And Other Stories   MARK TWAIN

Field Notes from a Catastrophe   Elizabeth Kolbert

THE FOUCAULT READER

ANIMAL,
VEGETABLE,
MIRACLE   BARBARA KINGSOLVER
WITH STEVEN L. HOPP AND CAMILLE KINGSOLVER

ELENA FERRANTE - My Brilliant Friend

Another client engaged Juniper Books to build a library that would be the center of their open–floor plan house. They did not have any books of their own that suited their vision for the library, so Juniper Books would curate them all. They envisioned the library as a central gathering place for the family and a decorative piece for a truly stunning home.

The bookshelves were the centerpiece of the home and the color scheme throughout was mostly neutral: black, white, cream, gray. When Thatcher reviewed the drawings sent by the designer—Stephanie Moore-Hager—from Dallas, he figured that they would want to continue the neutral palette onto the bookshelves for a serene look and perhaps have the books fade into the background so that all the other amazing design elements in the home could stand out.

Stephanie, however, had other ideas—she wanted the books to pop with color.

Part One

The client was interested in having fun and using whimsical touches around the house, why not make the books jump out instead of blend in?

As Thatcher and the Juniper Books team curated the book selections—about eight hundred books on requested subjects—and created renderings to show what the finished shelves would look like, they decided to color code sections by subject matter based on each member of the family's reading preference—Harry Potter, Lemony Snicket, and Mary Poppins for the daughter; Tom Clancy, golf, and travel for the dad; and books featuring art, wine, and food for the guests. Each book would be jacketed in pop art colors—golf would be green; wine and food, bright red; and the children's books, orange and purple. At the conclusion of the project, Juniper Books handed over a spreadsheet listing the books and a map of the shelves with a color key

included so that the family could find any book with ease.

When Thatcher finished shelving and arranging the books, he went across the living room to take a picture. He then looked at the image on the camera screen. From a distance and on the screen, the books didn't look like books at all. They looked like jelly beans, a whimsical touch that brought a sense of joy, play, and delight to the space. "How perfect," Thatcher thought. "Mind candy for the family and their guests to enjoy for many years to come!"

It doesn't take a large house, a large budget, or a new construction to be able to apply the principles we've mentioned here to any book collection or library.

As you look at your own books, think about why you have the ones you do and whether they are the right ones for you and who you are now. Then make a plan to methodically work your way through your books and through your house, one room at a time to transform your books into a storytelling vehicle that really brings joy and meaning to your life. We'll help you on the journey.

"All the books we own, both read and unread, are the fullest expres-sion of self we have at our disposal. . . . But with each passing year, and with each whimsical purchase, our libraries become more and more able to articulate who we are, whether we read the books or not."

—Nick Hornby[1]

FROM BOOK BURNINGS TO HOME LIBRARIES

Hornby's words on the previous page beautifully encapsulate both what we think a library *is* and *can* be for someone. Yet, this truth that feels so inherent and timeless begs the question: Were private libraries *always* so revelatory of one's character, so personal?

After the invention of Gutenberg's printing press, there was much greater access to books, yet the locus of control still remained mostly with church and state. At the beginning of the sixteenth century, monastic libraries were essentially the public libraries of the Middle Ages, as the larger religious houses served as the center of culture and education. In short, the church was at the cultural center of the axis for ideas and learning.

However, the monastic library system blew apart in 1536, prompted by Henry VIII's order for the Dissolution of the Monasteries, an attempt to separate the Church of England from its base in Rome, deemed necessary because two popes denied him his desired divorce from Catherine of Aragon[2] in order to marry Anne Boleyn.

In response to this dissolution decree and continuing Henry VIII's desire to sever England's connection to Rome with an even greater fervor, the commissioners of King Edward VI looted university, college, and monastic

libraries, utterly destroying their contents. It has been estimated that more than eight hundred monasteries were suppressed, and with them eight hundred libraries destroyed.[3]

Transfers of power tend to bring with them increased chaos and in this case book-burning reached a fever pitch. As documented in Geoffrey Moorhouse's *The Last Divine Office,* "Bonfires of books (ever a sign of something nasty on the march) flared up across the land, the more conservative bishops were replaced by men who rejoiced in flames."[4] How does one dismantle a culture? Dismantle the books.

Thankfully, not all books were burned as individuals stole them for their personal collections, and this selective theft helped protect countless historical titles from being lost forever.[5]

By the late seventeenth century, millions of printed books were in circulation. Auctions devoted to books began to pop up with frequency, each with their own printed catalogs, an indication of the further democratization of book collecting serving a more widely interested public. The idea of a "personal library" became possible, and started to transform toward the intimate space, as Nick Hornby describes, that we recognize today.

EXERCISE

....

Do I have a book collection, multiple book collections, or a library?

Take a look at your shelves all together. Do your books go together as one coherent library?

Now, look at your books individually. What are the stories you see? Do you have collections of books that are easily identifiable? Should you perhaps move some books closer together in order to tell a story with more impact? We will cover more steps about how to do this later in the book, but you can start thinking about your books and making changes now.

Maybe you decide to build a collection on a certain topic. *"I realized we're missing twenty books that Stephen King wrote in order to make our collection complete!"*

"I'm fascinated by stoicism and now that I can afford hardcover editions, I want to see how many I can find."

"Leather bindings of classic British spy novels are what I want. I'm going to find as many as I can and then find a bookbinder to make me more!"

"Female poets of the nineteenth century—that's my thing. Leather, hardcover, paperback, I don't care. I want as many I can find. The more obscure the better."

Maybe you discover that you now want a library, and if you have the space and the resources to build one you are very fortunate.

To paraphrase *Field of Dreams,* "Build the library and the books will come."

A Book, a Collection, or a Library?

Books as Art

WHEN THATCHER STARTED selling books in 2001, he mostly sold rare books and first editions one book at a time. However, within a few years, he was getting requests to curate libraries for interior designers and homeowners.

The requests were varied—one client with a home in South Carolina wanted a highly curated collection of contemporary books on different subjects in a number of rooms. Another client wanted a library of beautiful antique leather and vellum books for their home in Westchester County, New York. A spa in Miami wanted 1,200 white books to fill their shelves, creating a very modern and clean "Miami" look.

The designer for the Miami spa was Philippe Starck. Starck has been an innovator in the world of design for decades. His firm placed several orders in short succession for these "color walls" of books—black books for a project in Dallas, gold wrapped books for one part of a project in Panama, and vibrant rainbow colors for another part of that property. It didn't matter to these projects what the books were. The designer wanted a specific color and nice clean lines, with the spines left blank and no printed titles.

Juniper Books purchased thousands of sheets of high quality art paper to wrap the books in various colors.

As the blank books filled up the shelves at these client installations, Thatcher realized something. When the titles and colors of the original books melted away, what was left was a blank canvas made up of hundreds or thousands of books.

Could Juniper Books "paint" those canvases in a new way that the world had never seen before?

Thatcher had long understood the power of books to tell stories on their pages and on the shelves, but it was at that moment that he saw the true potential for artistic expression across the shelves.

Up until that point, Thatcher thought that his contribution to the world of books was to curate the best of existing books from sources all over the world. If a client wanted leather bindings, or oversize art books, or just nice clean hardcovers, he would source them and assemble them into a coherent collection. Occasionally he would work with clients on rebinding books, cultivating a network of bookbinders across the country. Because of this he knew how time consuming and expensive bookbinding was.

The epiphany about books as a canvas led to the invention of custom book jackets in 2008. The US economy was crashing, Juniper Books was seven years old, and Thatcher had a two-year-old son and a daughter on the way. It was a risky time to expand but Juniper Books moved out of the basement of Thatcher's house and into a 1,500 square foot warehouse.

Once there, Thatcher sat down at the computer with a stack of books next to him and a few hypotheses to test out:

Could book jackets be printed in a uniform color with their titles on the spines? Thatcher knew there would be a lot of demand from clients who wanted a specific color for their library but also wanted to be able to find their books.

Could old books be transformed into new-looking books with the addition of custom jackets? Conversely, could new books be made to look like old books with the addition of antique leather–style jackets?

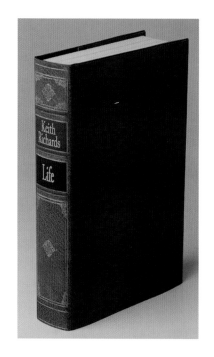

And lastly, could a group of books be pushed together to form a larger "canvas" on which art could be printed and displayed across the spines? If this was successful, the possibilities were endless.

Miraculously, all of these ideas worked and ten years later, Juniper Books produces hundreds of custom orders a year using each of these ideas, working with clients who want to do more with their books and their spaces,

to make their bookshelves come alive, to unleash their storytelling and artistic potential.[1]

Quite honestly, back in 2008 when printed book sales were declining, Thatcher also wanted to give people more reasons to buy books and keep them forever! Turning them into artwork was definitely one strategy worth trying.

Taking the three ideas that Thatcher started playing with in those early years and fast-forwarding to the present day, you can see the evolution of the company's design capabilities. Juniper Books invested substantial time and resources into determining what paper printed and folded best, how to make the jackets more durable, and what printers and other equipment to use in the process.

Viewing your books artistically and seeing your bookshelves as potential canvases for artistic expression can be a lot of fun. You can follow a similar approach that Thatcher took to the development of custom jackets as a transformative artistic medium.

The first idea from 2008 for printing custom jackets was all about color. The idea was to rapidly change the color of a whole shelf or wall of books from what the *publisher* had decided on for the color of the bindings or jackets to what *you* as the owner of the jackets really wanted. If you look at your bookshelves, how would you change the color of the books to suit your preferences?

Clients had been asking us for years to curate books with a specific color palette in mind, and white books and neutral color books were the most popular request by far.

Now the possibilities were endless and clients routinely ask Juniper Books to match a Pantone color, a carpet sample, or a paint chip. Is there a color in your home that you would match your books to if you had the chance?

The second idea that Thatcher had for custom jackets was all about changing the style of the books. In a nutshell, could we make old books look like new books and new books look like old books? Thatcher used his grandmother's grease-stained *Settlement Cook Book* for one prototype, making a brand new jacket for it, giving the book new life and presence.

For another set of prototypes, Juniper Books printed leather-style jackets for

autobiographies by Jay-Z and Keith Richards, turning them into instant classics that could stand next to Jane Austen and Charles Dickens.

What books would you transform in your home? Do you have old books that you'd like to make look like new? Do you have new books that you wish looked more like antique or vintage editions? Do you have a favorite binding or cover style that you'd love to get your favorite books in?

If you love Sue Grafton or John Grisham, would you want to transform them into leather-bound classics or Victorian novels

perhaps? Would you like your home to look like the library in *Downton Abbey*, but actually filled with the page-turners you love? Would you like to take the nonfiction you own and make it into a contemporary color library?

The third concept that we were playing around with at the inception of custom printed jackets was to print an image across multiple book spines. One of the first images that Thatcher experimented with was a self-portrait by Leonardo da Vinci!

Over the years, we've made hundreds of custom projects where we've printed

Part One

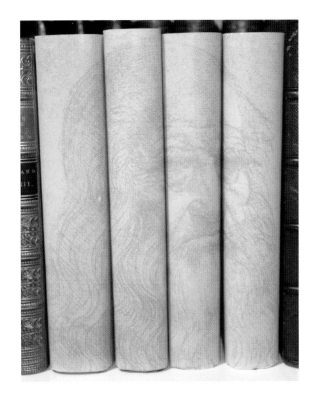

photographs, illustrations, original artwork, or reproductions of famous paintings across jacket spines—from a handful of books to more than 1,200 volumes.

Some of these projects are purely decorative with books that are not really meant to be read. The jackets are still wrapped around real books as we feel that the weight and depth of books conveys meaning even when the books are not intended for reading.

For the projects that combine very personalized book collections with personalized artwork, the combination can be magical.

Some people think it's superficial to make books look like anything other than the original publisher's binding. However, we would argue that by adding your own personal touch to the books, you are really making them your own. Further, it's a fact that you can't read all

"In the quiet spaces opened up by the prolonged, undistracted reading of a book, people made their own associations, drew their own inferences and analogies, fostered their own ideas. They thought deeply as they read deeply."

—Nicholas Carr, *The Shallows*

your books at any given time. We believe that your books should look great while they are on the shelves waiting to be read.

Turning the books you love into a work of art that is one of a kind may have deeper meaning to someone, we would argue, than owning a two-dimensional work of art. This work of art can be interacted with in so many ways.

You can take the books off the shelves and read them after all, the collection becoming a work of art that possesses hundreds or thousands of hours of entertainment, knowledge, and enjoyment.

If you were to transform your shelves into a work of art, what would you do?

Is there an image that comes to mind? A famous work of art that you would recreate? Or perhaps you would use your own photography or artwork extending across a group of books?

We've helped customers design custom color palettes, utilize custom typefaces they developed, print pictures by their children across the spines, and so much more.

Is this concept for everyone? Probably not. The nice thing about books is that there is something for everyone and you don't have to pick one style of books for your shelves.

Our bookshelves are artwork whether we go this extra mile or not. When we curate our book selections and choose how to present them on the shelves, they are already a work of art that reflects who we are.

We chose the books, we placed the books, we decided whether to leave them to entropy or keep them tidy.

You might think the authors wrote the books and the publishers designed the bindings, but those are individual works of creativity.

When you put the books together on personal bookshelves, the owner of those shelves is the artist. They are the storyteller.

Flipping Back
THE GENTLEMAN'S LIBRARY

With just about anything that can be collected—money, art, property—there comes a time when people with the means and the desire start to compete with their peers to see who can put together the best and largest collection.

It was inevitable that printed books would eventually follow this path. Handwritten manuscripts and scrolls had experienced this competitive drive before—in the service of power or religion—but in eighteenth- and nineteenth-century Europe, a fervor, bordering on obsession, gripped many to put together and display a library that was better than their noble peers'.

With the emergence of tastes inherent to the romantic period of the eighteenth century, coupled with the fact that books were now readily available to a wide-reading public, there was now the desire to set one's personal library apart from the rest, to showcase not just books, but *beautiful* books. As a result, book collectors began to collect leather-bound and antiquarian editions in earnest. As Charles Dickens recognizes in *Oliver Twist,* "There are books of which the backs and covers are by far the best parts."[2]

Enter the English tradition of the gentleman's library of the eighteenth and nineteenth centuries: wood-paneled marvels containing rows and rows of spines decorated in subtle tones of brown leather and illuminated gold-leaf lettering, the books comprising "all that well-brought up young man should know." If you were a fan of *Downton Abbey*, you are familiar with this concept. Lord Grantham's library would often steal the scene as we wondered what gems filled his shelves.

In nineteenth-century England, books were printed in softcover "wraps" then sent to the favorite binderies of each family to be bound per their instructions—preferred leather hides, colors, embellishments and decorations on each book, typefaces and title treatments, full leather, three-quarter leather, half-leather, endpapers, custom bookplates, and so on.

Most often the pages were left uncut, evidence today that the books were never read and they were just used for shelf decoration—and to make the families look smart!

What was the eighteenth and nineteenth century "gentleman" reading? Surprisingly, it's not very different from what we are reading now. You may find a small section of fiction, larger sections then devoted to history, biography, philosophy, poetry with plays and dramas sprinkled among a selection of atlases and travel accounts. Dictionaries and encyclopedias of "universal knowledge" were also prevalent in the eighteenth century library and not just one, but a variety—something we would rarely find on our shelves today.

The way a gentleman's library was organized is also not so different than the way we might organize our own, perhaps by subject, size, color—a system that was logical, personal, and made intuitive sense to the family. The next time you are touring a historical home—whether Edith Wharton's home, The Mount, or residence to British royalty, Windsor Castle, linger in the libraries and among the spines and think about what story the books tell about the occupants of yesteryear.

Where Art Belongs   Chris Kraus

HOWL   Allen

The Picture of Dorian Gray   OSCAR WILDE

WAITING FOR GOD   simone weil

FOREIGN AFFAIRS   Alison Lurie

RENATA ADLER SPEEDBOAT

NORA EPHRON   WALLFLOWER AT THE ORGY

WOOLF   A ROOM OF ONE'S OWN   HARCOURT BRACE JOVANOVICH

FORTY-ONE FALSE STARTS   JANET MALCOLM

Hopscotch Cortázar

cool for you   a novel   Eileen Myles

A LIFE FOR THE SPIRIT   HENRY BARNES

THE DIARY OF FRIDA KAHLO

THE MEN IN MY LIFE   PATRICIA BOSWORTH
A MEMOIR OF LOVE AND ART IN 1950S MANHATTAN

Books About Your Hobbies and Interests

THERE IS A BOOK about every subject. And there is a book for every person.

When Thatcher tells people about Juniper Books at a cocktail party, he's occasionally met with a response such as: "That's an interesting niche business but I'm not a reader so it's not for me."

The reality is that you don't have to be an avid reader or especially literary to have a book collection. If you are interested in a subject—cigars, knitting, travel—there is almost certainly a book about that subject, probably a handful or many more.

We would argue that it's actually possible to build a book collection on just about any subject! Perhaps you already have a collection of books about your hobbies and didn't even know it.

Over the years Juniper Books has curated collections of just about every subject under the sun. It's one of the things that makes the business so fascinating and never boring.

We love hearing about what people are interested in and pursuing the challenge of finding books for a set, a shelf, or a library on a particular topic.

Below are some examples of requests we have received over the years:

- Russian children's books
- Sicilian history
- Hollywood history
- Guitars
- The Space Race
- Harley-Davidson motorcycles
- Horseback riding
- Abraham Lincoln
- Marching bands
- Knitting
- Sheep
- German expressionist art
- Typography

There really is a book about every subject. Sometimes it takes just one book to begin a collection or to anchor a group of seemingly disparate books, providing a launching point to build a larger collection.

Two books can constitute a "collection." Once you have three, you're on a roll! The larger it is, the more it says that it's important to you and the more you can deepen your knowledge and immersion in that subject or hobby. Books are not just for readers or booklovers. Books are for everyone.

If you love a place—Italy or Amsterdam, for example—there are hundreds of books you could buy with beautiful photos to remind you of this passion. You can display them on your coffee table for all to see and you can revisit your travels every time you

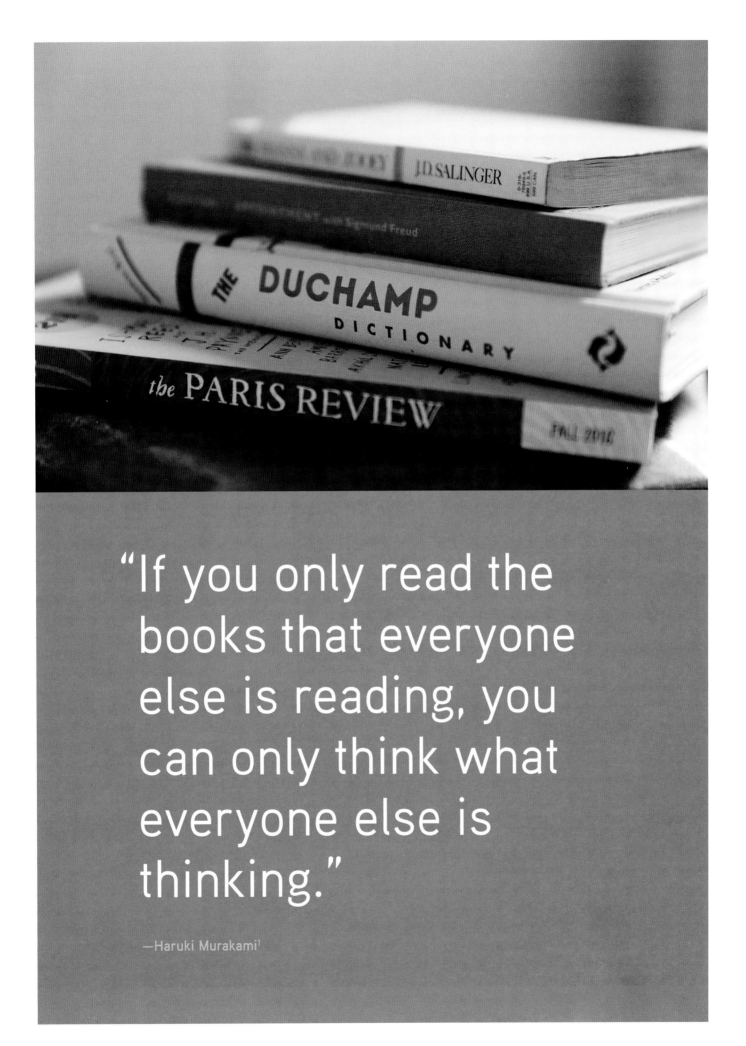

"If you only read the books that everyone else is reading, you can only think what everyone else is thinking."

—Haruki Murakami[1]

Part One

open the books. If you are interested in old watches or classic cars, there are endless publications that discuss their history in detail.

Do you hike? Enjoy time in nature? You could start with photography books about classic trails, expanding to Ansel Adams and John Muir. Then bring it back to fiction—perhaps Jack London's stories will be your go-to. Or find travelogues by Bruce Chatwin or Frances Mayes that you adore and must own in clothbound hardcovers or leather editions.

Do you love fine wine and great food? You could spend a small fortune on antiquarian books, rare early publications about cooking and wine making. Or find an endless supply of recent cookbooks, books about gastronomy, vineyards, and vintages. You could also focus on fiction and be entertained by Hemingway and Fitzgerald. The writings of M. F. K. Fisher and Jean Anthelme Brillat-Savarin are delicious to consume and if you have them on your shelves, it speaks to a certain seriousness about your interest in food.

Thatcher's Interests and Hobbies

My non-literary hobbies and interests in no particular order include: skiing, cycling, hiking, living in Colorado and the mountains, and Dartmouth College (where I went to school). Some of my favorite books in my collection are stories of Colorado in the nineteenth and early twentieth century.

My love of Colorado and the mountains led me first to stories of Colorado in the nineteenth century and one author in particular whom I became somewhat obsessed with—Enos Mills.

Mills is known as the "John Muir of Colorado" as he was instrumental in writing about and protecting the wilderness. He lived in Estes Park, Colorado, and lobbied for the successful creation of Rocky Mountain National Park. His books are filled with crazy adventures which he was often unprepared for. He encountered wildlife and extreme weather conditions in the Colorado mountains and wrote more than a dozen books. I wondered when I stumbled across the first editions of Enos Mills at estate sales why I had never heard of him before. Then I thought of how many authors and subjects there were similar to Mills, waiting to be discovered and collections of their works assembled.

Quite often books can be a vehicle for deepening your knowledge, interest, and passion for your hobby, something that could not have been pursued through the hobby alone. For example, you can love fashion and dress to the nines, but you can learn so much more about the history of fashion by reading a biography of Coco Chanel or flipping through one of the fashion house's coffee table books.

Books can open up unknown avenues and awaken interests, for that's their power. Trust it. Start where you are, with what you know and like, and then let the magic take hold.

Giving and Receiving Books

Not only is there a book or a collection of books for everyone, but non-readers tend to appreciate the thoughtfulness of receiving books that are in their interest areas. It's a considerate gift and it's wholly original, compared to the more typical host gifts of wine or flowers.

After all, if you know a cigar lover, you could try to buy them a cigar as a gift. But what *specific* kind of cigar do they like? Your taste or knowledge of the market may not be

as sophisticated as theirs. You don't really know what they already have in their cigar collection; what would enhance and what would simply be redundant or out of place?

However, gifting a book about cigars demonstrates that you know your friend, you've followed their interests, and thought about a gift that is meaningful, special, and not already on their shelves.

Soon after Thatcher started selling books and attending estate auctions, his dad, Barry

Wine, got the book-hunting bug alongside his son and would join Thatcher on his adventures. When they were apart (Barry lives in New York, Thatcher in Colorado), Barry would visit country auctions alone, often bringing home thirty or more boxes of books. He loved going through each box and finding the one gem amongst the many. When Barry attends a dinner or a party, he frequently brings a book as a gift for his hosts and, because he is a good observer of people's interests, he is often able to identify the perfect book for them!

For the most part, people are delighted to receive books as gifts, especially if the book is thoughtfully chosen. The level of consideration required to choose a book shows that you are both a thoughtful person and a good gift giver. If you are a good friend and a good listener you will know just what book your friend would love and appreciate—give them something that could become part of a cherished collection.

Where to Begin—Identifying Your Interests and the Collections You Already Have

Perhaps within your home you find yourself confronted with a different problem of space—too many shelves, too few books. Starting a collection can feel intimidating.

With more than 900,000 books published every year, when you begin to focus on your hobby or interests as potential book subjects, trust us—you'll find a book on that.

As you begin to go through your shelves, here are a few questions to ask:

Do you own some books in your interest area already?

Have you received gifts from people who knew you were into this subject and found a book for you?

How has knowledge and the treatment of the subject changed over time? Mixing new books on the subject with vintage and antique books is a fun approach.

Do you have stacks of books that you purchased and you aren't sure where to put them?

Did you previously tuck books somewhere random because you weren't sure if they belonged on the bookshelves?

Bring the piles into the light. You may find the undercurrents of a collection, unifying themes that you didn't realize you had!

EXERCISE

....

You have the shelf space and you want to fill your shelves with the books that are meaningful and authentic to you, yet where do you start? Start at the beginning. Keep it simple and ask yourself:

What are my hobbies? How are they represented in my home, but maybe not on my shelves? As you identify your interests, you may find you already have quite a few books on the subject.

Do I already own books on these hobbies? Can the books on the same subjects be brought together to tell a more impactful story?

Which of my hobbies are not represented on my shelves that should be?

Which of my hobbies are represented disproportionately? For example a hobby that I don't have any books on, or an interest that is overrepresented by too many books now that I'm not as into it as I once was?

Make a list of books and subjects you want to add.

Elevate Your Collection of Hobby Books

If you love Harley-Davidsons, does it make more sense to have a collection of books about Harleys or vintage road signs, or to perhaps mix the two? You could have a section of Harley books on your shelf and some Harley bookends holding them in place (they exist!).

If you love the Star Wars movies, you could buy a poster or some memorabilia at an auction, or even get a tattoo. All great choices. Building a book collection of Star Wars books on the other hand has different meaning, and could take up a lot of space as there are hundreds of titles. It's one of those fields with hundreds of series that can be collected on their own (e.g., the Rebel Force series, Adventure series, Jedi Apprentice series, etc.) or an attempt could be made at collecting them all. Once you collect all the American or English language books, you could move on to international editions. No matter what you do, the books you end up with will help tell the story of who you are to anyone who sees your shelves.

A few other ideas of collections to build around the house:

COCKTAILS: Maybe you have lots of useful books on the subject, recipes, etc., but perhaps a copy of the classic Savoy cocktail book would tie it all together.

LAWN CARE: Perhaps select a few how-to books from your region and couple them with a bit of inspiration from *The Education of a Gardener* and beautiful British landscaping books.

TRAVEL: You love Paris, but do you own a copy of *A Moveable Feast* or the works of Gertrude Stein?

The options are thrillingly endless; your library can flow in any direction.

When building a book collection and filling your house with books, it's inspiring to remember that you are the one in control of the book collection's destiny. It's not the creator of the series, the author of the books, or the publishing house—it's you.

You are the director, set designer, and storyteller for your shelves. You want the book and the reasons are wholly your own—to read, to possess, to display, for myriad reasons known only to you. You have a billion choices and, thankfully, the choice is yours—to choose *that* book and *that* place on your shelf.

COOKBOOKS, THEN AND NOW

One of Elizabeth's favorite hobbies is cooking (she even dreamt of going to culinary school). In lieu of a cooking career, she has built quite a cookbook collection and for about a minute in 2009, she thought her beloved reference text might be in peril. Could a genre with such a long history be proved irrelevant in the twenty-first century?

When one thinks of ancient books, generally the religious and philosophical variety come to mind first. But cookbooks, too, have a long and rich history. The first cookbooks, written on clay tablets 3,700 years ago were discovered alongside their more predictable counterparts and, similar to the texts of devotion we would expect, these early cooking texts are thought to have been created not for people, but rather for the gods.

In the Victorian era, the publication of *Mrs. Beeton's Book of Household Management* in 1861 caused a sensation selling nearly sixty thousand copies in the first year and nearly two million copies in seven years!

The other most successful cookbooks in history include the *Better Homes and Gardens New Cook Book* (nearly forty million sold), *Joy of Cooking* (eighteen million copies sold), and *The Fannie Farmer Cookbook* (originally called *The Boston Cooking-School Cook Book*)—with approximately four million copies sold.[2]

Fast-forward to the modern era: In the year 2010, as the printed book appeared to be facing its final days, none seemed closer to the chopping block than the hardcover cookbook. That stalwart home reference book seemed too cumbersome, perceived to be outdated as soon as it was printed, bordering on completely obsolete. The first iPad had hit the market and countless apps that would instantaneously download a digital shopping list from your favorite cookbook seemed like an answered prayer.

Apps from beloved websites like Food52 and Epicurious offered new ways to think about ingredients and recipes. They brought a library of books into the kitchen, loaded onto a single device that could be wiped clean after receiving a splattering of oil.

A sense of panic set in as publishers feverishly joined the app game, producing apps and enhanced e-books—multimedia marvels filled with beautifully staged food photos and user friendly how-to videos. There was some universal wonder about whether anyone would ever need (or want) to buy a printed cookbook again.

The iPad solved many of the printed cookbook's problems. Size was no longer an issue. A long ingredient list could now be easily managed. You could simply slip the ingredient list in your purse, no longer needing to physically transcribe. The app even sorted the ingredients by grocery store aisle.

However, instead of going away, printed cookbooks responded to the threat of technology by being upgraded. The cover designs got better, the quality of food photography dramatically improved, the content was richer and more engaging—the cookbooks printed today are rarely compendiums of recipes, they are often masterpieces of written and visual storytelling.

Similar to the magic of a children's book, there's that indescribable essence held within our favorite cookbooks, the ones with oil-stained pages and notes from our mother scribbled in the margins. With respect to technology, it's also possible we simply have user fatigue. Digital assistance in the kitchen while we are doing something very physically engaging—cooking, talking, and sipping a glass of wine—can be distracting and overwhelming instead of helpful. Flipping through a hardcover collection of recipes accompanied by beautiful pictures feels good; it nurtures our immersion in the world where we are present to do the cooking for, and feeding of, ourselves and our families.

Books for Children

THE MORE BOOKS you have at home, the better your child will do at school. That was the conclusion of two economists in 2010, Eric Hanushek and Ludger Woessman,[1] who analyzed student performance and households across international lines. The research was conclusive: if you have two bookcases in your home, the kids will perform well. It's not necessarily that they read every book in those bookcases, it's what having two or more bookcases in your home says about you and what is important to you and your family—education, reading, parenting, and so on.

We could just drop the mic here. Get some bookcases, fill them up, and everyone in your household will accomplish more in the world. But let's break it down into actual steps, to move beyond simply picking up a few bookcases from Ikea. Let's instead meaningfully fill them and bring a personal love of reading to the family, including the kids!

"Reading is the sole means by which we slip, involuntarily, often helplessly, into another's skin, another's voice, another's soul."

—Joyce Carol Oates[2]

Instilling a love of reading is giving your child a profound gift: of dreams, imagination, escape, connection, and empathy—that essential ability to see the world from a different perspective and walk in another's shoes. As adults, we ideally seek these shifts in perspective found in books somewhat intuitively. How do we foster this love of reading in our children?

The first step is simple. By merely choosing to keep books in our home we open up avenues of discovery and growth, even before we crack the spines to read. That stack of library books in the corner or the ones piled by our beds all possess a palpable energy that is uniquely a book's own. We've all felt this force contained between the covers of a printed book, indescribable, yet so very vital and present. And this energy only compounds once we begin to read.

When our children see us reading, they begin to follow our lead. They may begin this journey as babies and toddlers, leafing through our books as they pretend to read themselves, playing with the form of the book by tearing out all of the pages, or using their own board books as building blocks. The options are endless and each piece lays the foundation for a deep love of the printed page.

Elizabeth's Daughter's Library

When I was expecting my first child, my closest friend started our daughter's library with a few of her own favorite books from childhood, each book inscribed with a personal message. My daughter's favorite from this collection is Swimmy *by Leo Lionni, a book with which she presently feels a deep connection as she knows that it's been hers, on her bookshelf, since birth. She recognizes every tear, every crease, and bit of wear that comes with a book that (like that famous stuffed toy from* The Velveteen Rabbit*) is well loved.*

As my daughter has gotten older, she's planned the books she will pass on as an adult, carrying forward a love of books so beautifully represented in this first gift. She may not always hold the story of Swimmy *as close as she does now, the plucky fish who found her essential spot within the school. However, she will carry the context of the gift, that nugget that spoke to her as a young child when she understood this was her book, given to her by someone who loved her even before she was born. These feelings live on every time she looks to her bookshelf and sees that familiar, beloved spine.*

Building a library with a child can be one of the most rewarding and fun experiences for both child and adult. Those early independent reading years (from ages six to ten) are gold. Children begin to show great independence with regard to preferences, yet still value an adult's essential guidance. It's a time when kids are sponges, absorbing everything

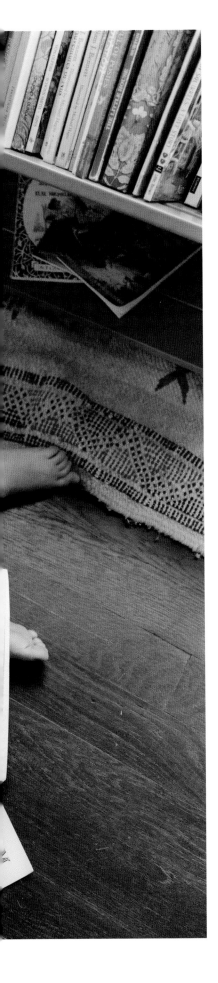

Books for Children

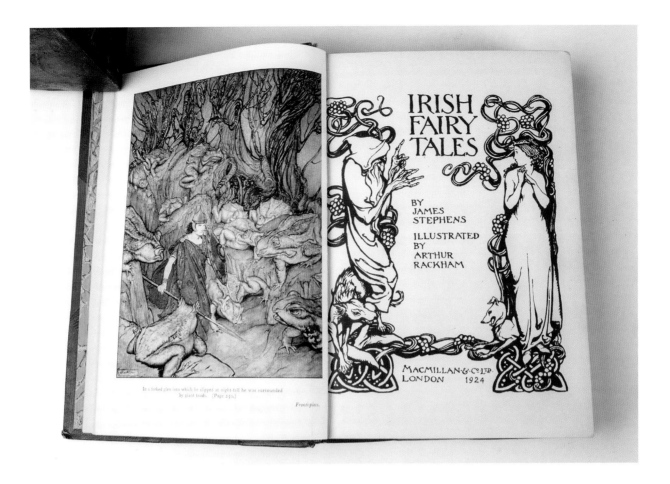

In a forked glen into which he slipped at night-fall he was surrounded by giant toads. (Page 250.)

Frontispiece.

around them and forming their own tastes, showing glimpses of who they will become.

While there exists a world of possibilities with regard to kids and reading, we know that it can feel daunting. Questions and fears abound. What if my child doesn't share my love of books? What if she only reads graphic novels for the rest of her life? What if he doesn't read anything at all? Ever?

As parents you want your kids to read and you want to balance your suggestions with an equal amount of stepping aside so they may discover what resonates with them—keeping a mindful eye, yet letting their own curiosity steer their choices. In this day and age, it's perhaps wise to put the brakes on technology use (such as playing a certain video game or spending time on social media), but it's rare that you would say "stop reading that book."

Maybe in the teenage years they start to read more things you aren't comfortable with. Do you stop them? Do you steer them away from reading so many vampire novels? Are we acting like the church or state banning certain books within the home?

It's a difficult question, and perhaps (as so many things do within parenting) falls to a case-by-case basis as we remember the flip side: telling someone they can't read a certain book only serves to make that title *more* desirable. If your children want to read something and you say no, they are far more likely to seek out a copy and hide it under the mattress, reading late into the night by flashlight—and is that so bad?

There is so much pressure as parents to do things right, and yet kids learn so much from us just being who we are, simply doing what we enjoy doing. If you love to read, let your kids see you reading. Kids home on a snow day? Let the kids play while you curl up in the chair with a mystery—it's a delight for you and for them.

One of the most magical things about books is simply that there are so many available to us, and with that comes the freedom to choose what to read. There is the perfect book, genre, style, and way to read for every child, even a reluctant reader. If we slow down and listen to their cues, we can then discover what they are naturally drawn to and what they like.

As adults we have a conception of who we want to be through our favorite books—who we are presenting to the world—and kids are the same. With kids, it is a fluid journey as they change their minds frequently, from Dr. Seuss to Roald Dahl and beyond. Let kids discover who they like (without boundaries) and don't be afraid if their stories are different than yours and if their preferences keep changing. Their sense of self will emerge from the experience.

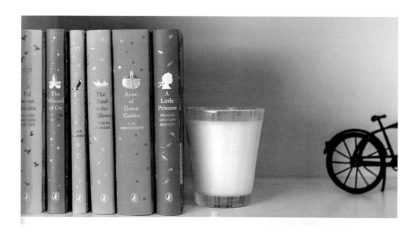

Books for Children

Tips to bring a love of reading to your child:

The following are practices learned from Elizabeth's reading experiments at home and her own early memories as a somewhat reluctant reader:

1. HAVE A FLEXIBLE READING HOUR EVERY EVENING

We started a new practice in our own household at the new year. Each night, the entire family heads to the living room for an hour or so. The only rule imposed is that it is a work-free zone for my husband and myself. No phones. No computers. Our girls may finish their own homework during this hour, but we adults are simply reading books that we enjoy. We (my husband and I) realized that we needed to do this first for ourselves,

to consciously carve out a little peace in the day with our phones turned off. As we committed to this practice, we noticed that our girls were picking up their own books and relishing this time spent reading as a family. It quickly became the most treasured part of our day and creating this space to read casually together (and also trusting that there *is* time to step away from work and the hustle of life) has been life-changing for us as we've discovered that there is always time to read for pleasure.

2. LET THEM READ, NO LIMITS!

I try to place no limits on what my girls read— and this tip was born out of my own childhood as well as my husband's. I absolutely

fell in love with reading when I was eight or nine years old, and my first love was one particular series—and definitely not a classic. I wrapped myself up in the Sweet Valley Twins series and books by Christopher Pike and John Bellairs. These books certainly weren't what my parents would have chosen for me, but they gave me the freedom to choose for myself and I dove in.

My husband had reading difficulties as a child. Because of this, no books were appealing to him and so his parents gave him the sports page instead. He loved it! Every day he would read the sports page, and through this practice he became a reader. It's in those moments, when a child is reading what *they* like that a lifelong reader may be born. So I say, let them read—no limits.

3. KEEP STORYTELLING ALIVE

Continue to read aloud with your children for as long as possible. Our eldest daughter is almost ten and we still read aloud together most nights, a tradition that I savor and hope will live on for several more years. My own children still love to snuggle in close and listen to a story. I find this is the perfect time to bring in those stories that have grown with us, such as classics like *The Secret Garden* or *Little Women*. Also, continuing to read aloud together, even in the preteen years, opens up one more avenue for conversation to blossom with our kids. It's a magical moment that's hard to outgrow, because it's just that: it's magic.

Part One

4. TURN "ME-TIME" INTO "READ-TIME"

My youngest daughter has a time in the day that she absolutely craves. She calls it "peace alone" and it was a concept she came to when she was only two or three years old. She is very social, and yet, for a few moments every day—it could be five or twenty minutes—she steals away to spend time by herself in the quiet. During this time she will do whatever she wants. She will play with toys, make up stories, lay on her bed just to stare at the ceiling, whatever fits the moment and the mood. As I watched my daughter grab these peaceful moments for herself, I realized how much we *all* need that. And so each day, I'll take five to twenty minutes by myself and my eldest daughter will now do the same. It's a time to find center, to settle into peace, and to relish the quiet. Each day brings with it more activities, more busyness, and with it, more noise. Yet, for the past few years we have sought out these quiet moments to refresh. The unforeseen side effect has been to create another natural space to reach for a book. As my girls started to crave the quiet and find space within these moments, they also found the space to expand into a story and into their own imagination.

5. CREATE NEW STORIES TOGETHER

My sister is nine years older than I am and when I was young she would often make up stories with me at bedtime. These were stories purely from her imagination and as she shared them I would weave in my own bits to add and enhance. We would watch as this creation would ebb, flow, and expand to endings unknown and often bizarre. We had so much fun with these stories, many of which I still remember today. My husband and I try to continue this tradition of story-telling with our girls—making up different tales, having them add their own twists and turns. These narrative wanderings help all of us tap into our creativity and fall more easily into our own imagination. And that's really when we fall in love with a story and its characters—when we can free fall into the world of the story through our own imaginings.

6. PUBLISH THEIR BOOKS

A while ago, my youngest daughter went through a seriously picky phase with food. Nothing was working and I'd reached the end of my own inspired ideas to get her to try the foods we were eating as a family. A friend of mine suggested that I bring her into the kitchen to cook with me, and it worked! The minute she felt that she had a hand in cooking our meal, she dove right in, eating with gusto! She felt pride in the preparation and so was excited to try the meal. With that experience close at hand, I realized the same might be true with reading. When the girls were first learning to read, we started writing stories and turning them into books—folding the pages, sewing the bindings. They created books, which meant they were authors! This cracked books open for them in a new way and made them more accessible. They realized they could create physical books similar to the ones on their bookshelves and so those books became relatable.

7. KEEP YOUR YOUNG READERS ON THEIR TOES

Revisit books your children loved as babies. Choose joke books to read or children's stories with the silliest humor. When you read aloud as they look over your shoulder, divert from the story into a crazy tangent—perhaps Mary Lennox opens the door to the secret garden and finds herself on the surface of the moon! Reading is play. It's leisure. It's recreation and it's fun. The more we can illustrate the play and the fun inherent in reading, the more kids will foster that outlook on their own and seek out space in the day to read.

8. DON'T STRESS ABOUT IT

This final tip is really one that I've gleaned from the times I've found myself wanting to do anything but read a particular book. Here's where the obligation to read trips me up every time: I am a part of a book club, and the minute our monthly books are assigned, my first impulse is to go rogue and read another book! It is such a silly reaction, but I know that in that moment I am rebelling against being told what to do. If it feels like homework, I rebel. My daughters often have the same instinct. So I try to keep it light, keep it fun, and if twenty minutes (or even five) isn't going to happen that day, I just let it slide.

THE INVENTION OF CHILDHOOD
AND CHILDREN'S BOOKS

The concept of "childhood" didn't really exist until the seventeenth and eighteenth centuries. Let us repeat that. Childhood, as a recognized phase of development, simply didn't exist. Children were seen as incomplete versions of adults. This viewpoint is amazing to contemplate today, with tens of thousands of parenting books and blogs guiding contemporary parenting. Because childhood was not viewed as a distinct state of being, there was no separate category of children's books or children's literature.

Early concepts of childhood slowly materialized in Europe in the seventeenth century as adults started to see children as distinct humans, wholly innocent and requiring an adult's essential guidance. In 1690, philosopher John Locke developed his theory of the *tabula rasa,* in which he posited that humans were born "blank slates" and our ability to process the world around us emerges solely from our sensory experiences. Taking this theory further to its practical application: since a child's mind was perceived as blank at birth, it was then the parent's job to instill the child with correct ideas.

Locke understood that children would respond to books that were fun and simple in both subject matter and tone, shifting the experience of gaining knowledge toward play rather than work—a distinctly progressive idea for the seventeenth century. Furthermore, Locke recommended adding illustrations to books, bringing even more joy to a child's learning experience.

With Locke paving the way for the concept of childhood, the modern children's book emerged in mid-eighteenth century England. *A Little Pretty Pocket-Book,* written and published by John Newbery in 1744, is considered the first modern children's book. A first of its kind, this volume sought to delight children with a mixture of rhymes, illustrated tales, and games. The book was smaller in scale (perfect for little hands) with a bright-colored cover that further spoke to a child's sensibility.

Following Locke's thread of influence further, the nineteenth century brought with it a shift in children's literature toward the humorous rather than didactic, stories that spoke more directly to a child's imagination.

Author Hans Christian Andersen traveled through Europe and gathered many well-known fairy tales, transcribing them in a way that resonated beautifully with a younger audience. The Brothers Grimm sourced traditional tales told in their native Germany. Grimms' stories found such an eager audience that realistic children's literature lost footing as stories of the fantastic took hold.

The availability of children's literature increased right in step with the greater numbers of books published in general. As children's literature grew as a genre, literacy rates grew in kind.

Works we still read to this day found their way to the shelves in the mid-nineteenth century: Lewis Carroll's *Alice's Adventures in Wonderland* (1865) and its sequel *Through the Looking-Glass,* Anna Sewell's *Black Beauty* (1877), followed by Beatrix Potter with *The Tale of Peter Rabbit* in 1902, to name a few well-known titles. And perhaps the most well known from America is L. Frank Baum's fantasy novel *The Wonderful Wizard of Oz,* published in 1900. Baum wrote fourteen more Oz novels, following the success of his first.

The longevity of these titles, and others like *Winnie-the-Pooh* and *Charlotte's Web,* is remarkable and speaks to the present day desire to collect classic children's titles. As such, rare and antiquarian children's books is a growing category among book collectors. Holding an antique children's book in your hands connects you to the children who held the book before you and perhaps to your own childhood as well—the books you held, how you felt, where you were, and other memories and emotions.

Well-loved and utilized children's books are often not in the greatest condition so there is a premium on finding copies that are not excessively worn, scribbled on, or damaged. Personally, we love coming across old books with signs of previous owners' use—names of the children who have owned the books, the occasions on which they were given, indications of their favorite parts of the books, and so on.

Old books tell stories and when we bring them into our homes and shelves, their stories merge with our own. That's the magic of books and book collections.

VEFA'S
KITCHEN

PHAIDON

MARGARITA
CARRILLO
ARRONTE

MEXICO
THE COOKBOOK

WHAT TO COOK & HOW TO COOK

SPAIN
THE COOKBOOK

I KNOW HOW TO   GINETTE MATH

PART TWO

domino Your Guide to a Stylish Home

GRACE A MEMOIR GRACE CODDINGTON

The Art of Richard Diebenkorn

WorkScape NEW SPACES FOR NEW WORK

The Living Room
TELLING YOUR STORY TO THE WORLD
WHO SEES YOUR BOOKS

ANYONE WHO SEES your library isn't just seeing the creative output of the authors who wrote the books. They are seeing the story of your life written across your shelves through the books that you've chosen to keep and display.

For most people, the living room is the main attraction for books at home. It is here that we tend to choose our *good looking* books, the books from our collection that shine and really show off who we are to guests in our home.

Most of the time, these aren't the books you are currently reading (those are in the bedroom or your tote bag). These aren't the books you use for reference; maybe those are in the office or kitchen. These are the books you want the world to see.

Elizabeth's Lesson in Bookshelf Styling

Several years ago, my husband and I moved to a house that had one wall with beautiful built-in bookshelves in the living room, extending from floor to ceiling. We eagerly lined up our treasured books and filled every inch—all the works of Kazuo Ishiguro and Ken Follett for him, the quasi-spiritual self-help sharing equal space with fiction for me. Yet, without intention, we also added a few other things to the bookshelf, simply because we loved them and we had more than enough space. We thought people would just see books on the bookshelves, rows of spines that would convey, in a generic sense, that we weren't just readers, we were booklovers. We didn't realize our friends would actually look at the books, the actual titles, and that we would then be reframed in their eyes because of these choices.

All this became clear during a party we hosted shortly after our kids started school. An acquaintance was looking through our shelves very closely (uncomfortably closely) and for an introvert like me, I felt like my soul was exposed. He landed on our complete boxed set of MacGyver *DVDs hiding on the bottom shelf—intended to remain out of sight. To my surprise, because of* MacGyver, *we are now good friends—all because of kinship discovered through Richard Dean Anderson.*

The moral? People love to check out your bookshelves. They will see every inch.

And so the task of organizing *these* shelves in particular—the shelves that face the world—can quickly become intimidating, for these books we've kept are also now the books we've chosen to represent us, our worldview, our very essence.

As you approach this space and these shelves, take a deep breath and dive in with a sense of delight and possibility alongside a healthy sense of theater and play. The narrative possibilities contained within the bookshelves are endless.

The living room is often the most visible room in the home. Some consider this the perfect spot for an active library where books are taken off the shelf with frequency, while others prefer a static presentation, like that of a painting on the wall or object on the mantle. In this case, there are often other spots throughout the house that reading occurs, like in bedrooms or kids rooms. Perhaps the coffee table in the living room serves as the spot for browsing.

"Books will grow in a house like a vine if you provide something to support them."

—Billy Baldwin[1]

One family approached Juniper Books because they had bookshelves in their living room that were sparsely filled with family photographs from their travels; they felt there was something more inviting and representative of themselves that they could do with this space. They asked Thatcher if it was possible to create an installation across the shelves with books displaying photos of fourteen places they loved to visit on the spines.

Juniper Books created custom jackets to reflect this vision, using some of the family's own photographs alongside other stock photography. Once the shelves were installed, the family quickly found that the books served as a conversation starter, bringing their loves and interests to the forefront of conversations.

A different approach can be found on the shelves in the home of Gwyneth Paltrow. Gwyneth was a childhood friend of Thatcher's, however they had not spoken in the decade preceding the publication of Gwyneth's cookbook *My Father's Daughter*. Thatcher happened to have an amazing photo of Gwyneth and her dad dining at his parents' restaurant—The Quilted Giraffe— in the 1980s. He used that photo to make a custom jacket for Gwyneth and sent it to her wrapped around her book as a gift. The two got back in touch and have collaborated on special gifts, books for Goop (Gwyneth's lifestyle brand), and selections for Gwyneth's home over the years.

Gwyneth's family room functions as the heart of the house. It's the room in which everyone spends time together, where the

Another example of an approach to building a library was that of a family who met with Thatcher after the patriarch of the family, a successful entrepreneur, had passed away. Three generations of the family still spent time in the house, but going into the grandfather's office was associated with loss and sadness. Everyone associated the room only with him. The matriarch invited Thatcher to transform the space, hoping to create a library that multiple generations would want to use, a space where every member would feel welcome. In addition, the family had built their business around education and reading—what better way to honor the patriarch of the family than with a library of books to encourage his family to learn, explore, and enjoy the power of storytelling.

It was a large room, so Thatcher first recommended ways to break up the space into different thematic collections. One section would be devoted to the younger members of the family with children's books and classics lining the shelves, another section for history, followed by travel, culture, and finally, art books.

One of the most magical spots was where the patriarch's desk used to stand, the very place that had seemed unapproachable. A game table was placed there, where the grandkids could gather to play cards, tell stories, and laugh. Juniper Books made custom books for the nearby shelves with images of playing cards and with card game rules printed on the jackets, a fun, one-of-a-kind custom set.

The room became a true reading library, one that is actively used and enjoyed. The transformation was made possible with books. More than simply completing the family's story, this family needed a way to *begin* to tell their story by changing the very perception of the room. By mapping out each area of the room and filling each section with books that told a specific story, the family finally felt invited into the space—first to read, then to share and participate in the space with each other, taking books off the shelf, playing games, and sparking new conversation.

From these examples, the following advice emerges: Don't just fill your shelves. Think about your *intention*—what you are trying to accomplish with the books that you keep and display, and what story would *you* like to tell in a particular space about you and your family?

Remember, one room doesn't have to tell the whole story. Feel free to break your story apart and spread the narrative through different spaces, carrying the essence of you and your entire family throughout the home.

Books visible: AYN RAND, BOB DYLAN, BOB DYLAN LIVE 1975, Diary of a Genius · Salvador Dali, BHAGAVAD GITA, THE UNTETHERED SOUL, The Yoga Sutras of Patanjali · B.K.S. Iyengar, Light on Yoga, THE DEATH OF IVAN ILYICH, THINGS FALL APART, STORIES · PAUL BOWLES, AA Gill is away, A RETURN TO LOVE · Marianne Williamson, JUST KIDS · PATTI SMITH, WAR · ART, Waging Heavy Peace · NEIL YOUNG, Sally Mann · Hold Still, The New American Spirituality · Elizabeth Lesser

I LOVE MY FAMILY

Books visible: THE ART OF SIMPLE FOOD, PLENTY · OTTOLENGHI, POLPO, SUNDAY SUPPERS · KAREN MORDECHAI, SAM & SAM CLARK · MORO EAST, EVERYTHING I WANT TO EAT · Koslow

Books visible: CENTURY OF THE CHILD, TANTRA SONG, ART OF ATTENTION · Franck André Jamme, DESIKACHAR · THE HEART OF YOGA, 1 SHOCK MYSELF, THE COLOR OF HORSES, THE BIRTHDAY BOOK, Living Passages for the Whole Family, A BEAUTY COLLECTED, GREY, A COURSE IN MIRACLES, THE SPELL OF THE SENSUOUS, GRACE · A MEMOIR

Books in the Kitchen

DO BOOKS IN THE KITCHEN really require a separate chapter? Don't you just put the cookbooks on the counter and then you're done?

Yes, but . . .

As with all the books in your home, there are benefits to bringing a little more thought and complexity to this area.

The kitchen is often the living, breathing heart of the home—the place to create, connect, and gather. It is this room in which we often spend the most time and the one which holds the most memories.

Anyone who's ever hosted a party knows that guests love to crowd in the kitchen. It becomes the living room when you're entertaining, so why not bring books in and have a little fun? Take the books beyond the instructional reference books just for cooking.

The books in Elizabeth's kitchen follow the theme of food, yet the genres extend beyond cookbooks to include fiction, mcmoir, poetry, and children's books—anything with a connection to food or dining. This creates a space that is unique, one that tells her own story alongside the family's story. This type of complexity adds more to what makes a kitchen great—conversations held within a space that reflects who we are and expands connections with our friends.

Requests for Juniper Books to create something different with books in the kitchen don't come every day, but when they do, we try to work closely with clients to maximize the opportunity to be unconventional. Perhaps it's related to Thatcher's father, Barry Wine, and his unconventional career in the kitchen!

Barry graduated from the University of Chicago Law School in the 1960s, practiced law on Wall Street, then moved upstate New York, and later opened a restaurant as a side venture. He went on to become one of the most innovative and celebrated chefs in New York City, overseeing The Quilted Giraffe. The lack of formal culinary training or being bound to a particular tradition allowed him to come up with new ideas for the restaurant including dishes such as the Raw Tuna Wasabi Ricotta Pizza (still served at The Mercer Kitchen in New York).

Books in the Kitchen

Food and books are two incredibly important things in our lives that can be sourced from all over, remixed into infinite combinations, and presented in ways no one thought possible. A few decades ago, perhaps most people thought that dinner was dinner. Now there are entire TV networks, magazines, blogs, and more, constantly creating and repackaging dinner as we know it!

The same goes for books—they have not experienced quite the same media revolution as food, but they hold the potential to yield as much or more delight and entertainment in our homes. If we open up the possibility of play with our books, we can have a lot of fun and learn more about ourselves and the world.

Cookbooks are one of the most used books in the house—constantly pulled off

the shelf, thumbed through, dog-eared, and spilled on. They are the workhorse books, wearing the evidence of their use on their covers and pages. Historically, these books were mostly information and text.

Think of your family's well-loved copy of *Joy of Cooking* or *Cook's Illustrated;* or books by Julia Child and James Beard. These books were and still are the cornerstones of many kitchen cookbook collections.

Recently, though, there has been a shift as cookbooks have become art books in their own right, lavishly illustrated with elaborate covers, beautiful food styling, and photography. Just like books of a variety of genres might find their home on the kitchen shelves, a cookbook can now live beyond the kitchen counter, moving to the dining room or even your living room.

Elizabeth has a few cookbooks piled on her bedside table, in her living room and dining room, and all throughout the house really. In her mind, cookbooks belong everywhere. And yet, even with these design upgrades and genre-bends, the way we use our cookbooks is essentially the same. These books yearn to be used.

Thatcher's kitchen library contains a variety of cookbooks from Jewish to gluten-free to the healthy recipes that got him and his family through cancer treatment in 2017. The books from this period, when Thatcher was mostly unable to cook while going through chemotherapy, have additional meaning to him post-cancer. The books symbolize a time in life that was difficult; keeping the cookbooks that helped him get through that time is part of his story.

Small Victories

For many families, the books in the kitchen tell the story of family history through various cuisines. When Juniper Books curates cookbooks for a family, we ask about the family history and their culinary preferences, trying to get a sense for how they will interact and be inspired by the books.

Some clients have a collection of cookbooks they own and love, and they can send them to Juniper Books to have them wrapped in a design that unites the books while enhancing the decorative aspects of the kitchen. A nice clean look for the jackets keeps the books white with the titles revealed as a subtle decorative element on the spine, complementing the neutral tones of the space while also making sure the books are easy to access and reference.

Look at your kitchen with the fresh eyes of an artist—seeing both the space and the negative space. Within each there are endless possibilities.

The shelf at the bottom of your bar cart? A perfect spot for books! The corner of your countertop? More books! That mortar and pestle you thought you would use more, but haven't? A bookend! That odd space between your cabinets and the ceiling? Line it with books!

Your favorite foodie fiction will fit easily alongside the Michael Pollan classics, and Tomie dePaola's *Strega Nona* is a natural fit alongside Russel Hoban's *Bread and Jam for Frances* and Elaine Dundy's *The Dud Avocado*. The point is, within this space freedom reigns. There are few rules, so let's have some fun!

Bend the rules, play, stack the books high in the usual (or unusual) places, extend the boundaries, and fall in love—with food, with conversation, and community; with the space; and most importantly, with the books that bring it all together.

Part Two

BEER   WINE   WHISKEY

Practical tips for creating a kitchen library

📚 Keep your most used cookbooks on the lower shelves, stored vertically so that they are easily within reach.

📚 Turn the spice rack into cookbook storage with a face out display.

📚 Use a vintage milk crate to store cookbooks on the countertop or a vintage dish rack for kitsch appeal.

📚 Store books beneath the kitchen island.

📚 Utilize just about anything to serve as a bookend, even a favorite bottle of olive oil.

📚 Use the empty space above the refrigerator or above the cabinets for more books.

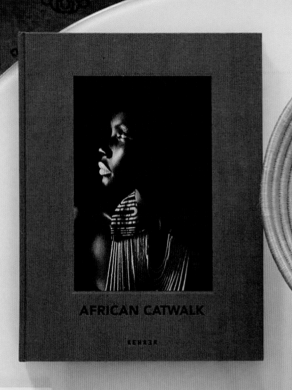

AFRICAN CATWALK

KEHRER

KERRY JAMES MARSHALL
Mastry

REMIX

DECORATING WITH
CULTURE, OBJECTS, AND SOUL

Jeanine Hays & Bryan Mason
founders of AphroChic
PHOTOGRAPHS BY PATRICK CLINE

Books in the Dining Room and Alternate Spaces

IN OUR HOMES TODAY, especially in cities, space is often at a premium. This is when we find that books move into spaces beyond the usual or expected, such as the kitchen or the dining room. Bringing books into these other spaces might feel unusual, yet wherever a book enters the scene, a sense of warmth, coziness, and conversation is sure to follow.

With few exceptions, books tend to make a space more inviting and grounded—more like home. Books help your guests settle within your own four walls even if they can't pinpoint exactly why they feel so at ease. It's the books! They serve as signs declaring, "This is a lived in space."

Go into a number of restaurants and it is immediately evident that it's hip to have books as part of the decor. When the NoMad Hotel opened in 2012, the developer (Sydell Group) and the operators of the restaurant—Will Guidara and Daniel Humm—had a vision to populate the shelves of the bar with hand-selected books.

They didn't want to just carelessly fill the shelves like many other hotel lobbies and restaurants had done before; they wanted to curate subjects that made sense and felt relevant to their clientele.

Guidara and Humm worked with Thatcher and Juniper Books to create a plan for the library around several themes including books about food and drink, New York, France, and living the good life.

The result of these approximately 1,400 curated selections is that the books are additive to the decor, soothing, and feel like they belong. It is evident that someone paid attention to the books. Each one has a place, rather than the books chosen in bulk as "filler," which would ultimately detract from the restaurateurs' intention.

Soon after opening, the library was always full and the hotel had to expand into the property next door to accommodate hotel guests and everyone who wanted to hang out in the library. While the design, food, and service contributed the most to its popularity, we'd like to believe that the books also played a part. When you are in a space where someone has paid attention to the details and everything feels like it belongs, you feel like you belong there too.

The books we choose to bring into these rooms should add to the experience, rather than distract and take you out of your own experience with the food or the company. In the NoMad library, a guest could browse the shelves and feasibly find a title of interest to

Books in the Dining Room and Alternate Spaces

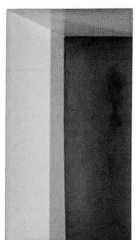

them, as if that book was chosen with them specifically in mind.

If there is intent in the selection of books, it instantly puts guests at ease—whether in a home, a hotel, or restaurant. Placing books in unexpected places, such as the kitchen or the dining room, can be a perfect conversation starter. When Elizabeth is at someone's house and at a loss for words she often turns to their bookshelves, finding a question to ask within the stacks. This tactic can be an introvert's savior!

In a dining room, bringing a few books about food, wine, and drink out of the kitchen and into this space makes perfect sense. It is also a great place to feature fashion, art, and photography books as shown in the Los Angeles dining room pictured here. The books in the dining room don't have to have any connection to food if you don't want them to, they can be conversation starters or just an extension of your library in another room.

Part Two

To the Lighthouse
The House of the Spirits
Catch-22
Nineteen Eighty-Four
My Ántonia
The Adventures of Augie March
Love in the Time of Cholera
Speak, Memory

A Passage to India

Beloved

Books in the Dining Room and Alternate Spaces

SHADES of GREY   KATE WATSON-SMYTH

BLACK & WHITE (and a bit in between)

MARILYN MONROE A LIFE IN PICTURES

NATURALLY NOURISHED

GJELINA

Books in the Bedrooms

THERE ARE A LOT of rules about what to keep in the bedroom and what not to keep. Sleep is important. Now we're
told by experts to turn off our computers and phones, and
not use them just before going to bed. All these devices
emit "blue light" which confuses our circadian rhythms.

While some experts might say that one shouldn't even
read printed books in bed because of the potential dis-
rupted sleep, a true booklover knows that a book is often
an insomniac's best friend. On whichever side of the fence
you land—books or no books before bed—it's a great idea
to have at least a few books in your bedroom, guest rooms,
and kids rooms; a place to fill the shelves with your personal favorites and stack your to-be-read pile high!

The books in your bedroom are generally what you are
reading *right now* and probably don't need to be as organized as the rest of the house. With current reads, you
might not yet know where the book fits into your overall
story—is this book a keeper? If so, which collection should
you group it with?

You won't find many softcover books in Thatcher's house except in the bedroom, and there you will find a stack of them on the nightstand, another stack on the floor, and a few on the shelf next to his writing desk. There's not much styling of the books there; they are pretty functional and meant simply to be read.

Some clients place bookcases or install built-in bookshelves in their bedrooms and want to have more privacy for certain collections. If the living room and kitchen shelves are really where you display the story you want your guests to see, the bedroom is where you can keep the story to yourself. It can be completely different from what you project to the world, but nonetheless it should inspire you to read, remind you of the subjects you love, and offer an alternative to powering up the TV or your device.

Part Two

Tips for Keeping Books in the Bedroom

📚 Maintain some variety: Have a few books in your favorite genre (if it's contemporary fiction, for example), but then consider keeping books outside of the norm to keep things interesting.

📚 Keep at least three books next to your bed: Read before you go to bed and if you have trouble sleeping, reach for a book in the middle of the night instead of your phone. There are great rechargeable book lights available, so that your partner can sleep in peace while you read into those wee small hours.

📚 If you feel like staying in bed after you wake up (and can do so) during the week, or on weekends when you have a bit more time, try it! Stay in bed and read a couple chapters before starting your day. It's an amazing little luxury.

📚 Invite your partner and kids to read in the same room or in their bedrooms at the same time. Turn off the TV and devices, and just have quiet time.

📚 If a book has been on your bedside table for a certain amount of time without your picking it up (let's say: three months), then maybe it's time to donate it or trade it in. Move a different book to the same spot and see if it compels you to read it!

📚 Sometimes it's overwhelming to have a stack of unread books that you see day in and day out, and don't make any progress on. Don't get discouraged; you have to start somewhere. Start at the beginning of one of the books and try to make a new daily habit to read in small increments.

Books in the Bedrooms

Books in the Children's Rooms

CHILDREN'S BEDROOMS ARE a bit of a different case than their adult counterparts, as it is often solely in the kids rooms that their own books are stored. Many clients have come to Juniper Books looking for guidance for their children's libraries. We frequently curate collections of the classics and the books that parents and grandparents read and loved as kids: *White Fang, The Merry Adventures of Robin Hood,* and *Aesop's Fables* among others. We also build collections of more recent award-winning books—it's hard to go wrong with selections of Newbery and Caldecott Medal winners, for example.

What J. K. Rowling and Harry Potter have done to inspire a reading habit among recent generations is amazing. The series has sold more than five hundred million copies. Beyond just being great stories in and of themselves, the Harry Potter series has also created a passion among readers for their specific copies of the books! *Harry Potter* is not a book that you read and then give away. Fans keep their books forever, re-read them, and proudly display them.

Part Two

there was a way to stick the books to the wall, above the bed? With this system, Jasmine's favorite books would always be within reach, fun to put back, and serve as a focal point for the room's decoration.

Thatcher commissioned a metalworker to make an L-shaped magnetized shelving system to install in Jasmine's room. Then Thatcher glued magnets to the back of Jasmine's favorite books. After reading one of these books they would just stick the book to the wall!

Jasmine had so much fun sticking the books to the wall that putting the books back in their proper place became a fun game. When Jasmine and her dad got tired of certain books or discovered a new favorite, they'd rotate the collection by installing a magnet on the new book. Jasmine could choose to display any books she wanted, thus truly telling the story of who she was, even at age three, with the books on display.

One client framed the covers of her daughter's favorite books to display around her room, while another built a high shelf on which to display her son's beloved set of Harry Potter books. There are no limits to what might transpire with a little ingenuity and a burgeoning love of books.

Feel free to use your reading time as experimental grounds to make improvements and innovations in your young one's reading space. Stack books in new ways, stick them to the walls . . . the ideas are endless.

Quick Tips to Organize Your Child's Library

📚 Change it frequently.

📚 Organize it with your child in different ways—by color, by size, by subject. See what they respond to and if they like seeing the patterns on the shelves ("All three of those books have bears in them!").

📚 Keep sentimental favorites even as they are outgrown, perhaps on a high shelf, or consider framing them. When your child grows up, they will remember these books and how they were important to who they were and who they are.

📚 Observe how your child reads the books and places the books, and try to support them on their reading journey.

PART THREE

asimov | Foundation and Empire | Panther Books 13555

THE NEW COLLEGE LATIN & ENGLISH DICTIONARY

The KITE RUNNER

PICTURES
LIFE WITH AUTISM | TEMPLE GRANDIN

TONI MORRISON | 0-452-26446-4 FICTION

ATION | AMIS

ONICLE | MURAKA

Ian McEwan

LUCKY JIM by Kingsley Amis

JOYCE MAYNARD | LABOR

HOW TO APPEAL TO MAN'S APPETITES

Animals in Translation

JOHN le CARRÉ | A Delica

MARY OLIVER NEW AND SELF

ZADIE S

A FINNE BALAN

A Man in Full | TOM WOLFE

IN THE DESERT

OF CANNAE

MOLE PEOPLE

ESE FOR BUSY PEOPLE

What Stays and
What Goes

WE'VE ALL BEEN THERE. The moment you are staring at your bookshelves and your eyes land on that book—the one that you can't believe still sits on your shelf. You should have given it away ages ago. In Elizabeth's case it was *Little Girl Lost* by Drew Barrymore.

No offense to Drew Barrymore, but how had this book traveled with Elizabeth—through college and all the moves post-college—and ended up here, on the living room bookshelf no less, almost three decades later?

Your own discoveries may not be quite as stuck in time as Elizabeth's, but there will be opportunities to cull your books, as you reflect on who and where you are now.

You're ready to refine your collection of books, but where do you start? Full bookshelves can feel overwhelming. Now is the time to keep it simple as this process is both physical and emotional. Start with one shelf and take baby steps as you work your way through all your books.

Let a sense of ease dictate this phase. When you select the books that may no longer make sense in your home, a sense of space and lightness should come with the process.

Don't worry about placement at this point, simply move through your books and decide which oncs still resonate.

Perhaps you will come across a beloved paperback that should be upgraded to a hardcover or first edition. You might find a hardcover that no longer reflects your story and should be donated. Sometimes you'll discover a series of books that you'd forgotten about which feel intrinsically linked to who you are. Some decisions will be made quickly, some will take more time and soul-searching.

As you scan your titles and remove the books that don't belong, we aren't going to ask you to hold each one and see whether it *sparks joy,* as Marie Kondo asks. You could if you want to, but our relationship with books is usually a bit more complicated. You may feel one way about the content, but have a different attachment to the binding, the context, where you received it, and what part of your story this books reflects.

"A book is not only a friend, it makes friends for you. When you have possessed a book with mind and spirit, you are enriched. But when you pass it on you are enriched threefold."

—Henry Miller[1]

Here are three questions to ask yourself as you decide what stays and what goes:

DOES THE BOOK BELONG IN MY LIFE AT ALL? Take away what should be removed. These books (we all have them) should find a new home. Make a stack of books to donate, trade, or sell. See later in this chapter for ideas on where to take them.

DOES THE BOOK BELONG IN MY LIFE, BUT JUST NOT RIGHT HERE? Make a stack of these books and perhaps put a sticky note on them to define where in the house they should go—your office, the kitchen, or maybe just in a box in the garage.

DOES THE BOOK BELONG IN MY LIFE, BUT JUST NOT THIS EDITION? There are a lot of stories that we want to have around, but as we move and our design sensibilities evolve, we may want nicer things. An example of this might be your college paperback edition of *I Know Why the Caged Bird Sings*. You adored Maya Angelou, but there must be a nice hardcover edition of the book you loved so much that would look better in your living room. Set these books aside in a separate stack and label them: "To be upgraded!"

Once you've gotten these easy picks—the low hanging fruit—out the door, take another pass. This culling will be a bit harder, as it will take some time to discern why you may be holding on to a particular title.

When you ask yourself the "why" behind each book, you will start to see your collection with fresh eyes. Notice the books you bought in college, or during a spiritual quest in your twenties, or those how-to books about home renovation that fill an entire corner of your shelves. Take stock of the poetry books, knitting books, book club books . . . all the Tom Robbins books purchased to impress a partner. These may be experiences you no longer wish to revisit.

Recognize who you are right now and also where you are headed. Are these titles still relevant? If they're not, send them into the world where they will have new meaning for someone else. They have already served their purpose for you. Set them free and move on.

When you feel a certain pull or repulsion, ask yourself:

"Is this part of my story or is it ancient history?"

"Am I truly reflected in this stack of college-required reading: the Kafka and the Nietzsche?"

"Are these ten recent presidential biographies that I read and enjoyed a more accurate reflection of who I am in this moment?"

Trust the answer.

Some books may still be a part of your story, yet they too may not belong on the shelves. Thatcher has books that fit this category and so he keeps them, just not in the bookcase. Instead, he stores them in file boxes. These books may be ones he will give away at a later date or they will find their way back on the shelves. Their fate is not yet written in stone and that's OK.

Once you have a few boxes filled with potential donations, check each book again to make sure that it is fit to donate. If any of the books are dirty, moldy, burnt, water damaged, missing covers or pages, have damaged bindings, or excessive writing, markings, or highlighting, please responsibly recycle them.

Boulder, Colorado, is fortunate to have a place called the Eco-Cycle Center for Hard-to-Recycle Materials which recycles books (and lots of other items). A few phone calls around your local community will hopefully yield ideas on where to take your books. Perhaps the local library can advise on who recycles books.

Here's a good rule of thumb: If the books aren't in good enough condition to give to a friend, recycle them.

As the quantities of books on your shelves get smaller, you will probably feel a new energy that the shelves now bring to the space and it will become easier to discern what stays and goes. Let the shelves speak to you and follow your intuition.

After you've determined which books no longer belong in the room you are working on, it's time to take another look at what remains and confirm you actually have

what belongs. Maybe you do this after taking a lunch break or on an entirely different day in order to see things with fresh eyes.

Going through your books, parting ways with some of them and soul-searching for the meaning of the others, can be physically and emotionally draining. If that happens, remember it's a healthy process to go through. Roll through it with grace. Books are meaningful. They are objects that may have been with you a long time and you may have deep, somatic memories of where you have been together.

Some time and space may be required to go through all your books. It's OK to take a break and not tackle it all at once. But don't delay too long. The risk is that if you never go through your books—absorbing their energy and revitalizing your connection to them—you may get to the point where you no longer have the energy to do so in this lifetime.

Don't let your books become like Charles Foster Kane's sled in *Citizen Kane*! The cinematic masterpiece by Orson Welles opens with the mysterious last word of the dying wealthy newspaper magnate, "Rosebud." Rosebud, we discover as the story unfolds, is the name of Kane's beloved sled, incinerated by Kane's household staff after his death. They are unaware of the meaning it had in his life. Kane longed for the innocence of childhood that the sled represented, but he died without ever sharing the personal meaning the object held for him.

Your books are part of your story and you are the one who knows your story best. You should recharge the story you want to tell on your shelves and make it known to the world while you can still enjoy it and while you have the vitality to do so!

If Kane had just taken the time to place the snow globe he held as he died on a

bookshelf earlier in life, next to his favorite childhood books and perhaps with the Rosebud sled leaning against the wall, we would argue that his life would have been much happier and more fulfilling. He would have understood that these objects, and the memories they were attached to, held meaning. Perhaps he could have placed them in context in a way that others could have understood him more fully. There is power in all forms of storytelling and we do believe that books are visual objects of storytelling.

Once you have gone through your books and figured out what to part ways with (and perhaps detoured to contemplate your own mortality without becoming immobilized!), it's time to think more deeply about why you are keeping what you are keeping.

REASONS TO KEEP BOOKS

TO READ THEM ONE DAY! If you hope to read the book one day, definitely keep it. It's fine to be aspirational; no one else will keep score on what you have actually read. It's great to dream and hope that one day you will have the time to read all your books.

TO TELL YOUR STORY. Some people give away every book they've read explaining, "What's the point in keeping a book after I've read it if I'm not going to read it again? It's someone else's turn to read my copy now." If that works for you, then only keep books on your shelves that you haven't read yet. However you can probably understand that the books that you haven't yet read only tell the story of your future, they don't say much about where you've been and what made you who you are today.

TO MAKE PEOPLE THINK YOU'VE READ THE BOOK. This one may be hard or easy for you to admit, but we don't think there is any shame in it. Sometimes we hold on to books because they represent our aspirational selves, supporting the perception of how well read or intelligent we are. They are certainly the books our ideal selves would read, but in reality—if we had to admit it—we probably never will. We would argue that you should still have these books around. They are part of your story and who you want to be.

TO INSPIRE SOMEONE ELSE in your household to read those books one day. Perhaps it's your kids or maybe your guests. Keeping books for the benefit of others is thoughtful and generous. At the very least, anyone who comes into your home will know that these are important books and will be exposed to the subjects and authors that you feel are important. Whether they actually read Charles Dickens or just know that he existed and was a prolific writer after seeing your books: mission accomplished!

TO RETAIN SENTIMENTAL VALUE. People keep a lot of things that have sentimental value: photographs, concert ticket stubs, travel knickknacks. Books, we would argue, have deeper meaning as sentimental objects. That childhood book of your grandmother's—she may have spent hours and hours with it and perhaps it was instrumental in her education. That is much more impactful than a photograph or a ceramic figurine. You are holding in your

hands what she held in her hands. This brings her into the present and into your home, taking up space on your shelves and acknowledging the thread of family and history that unites you. Books can do that in ways that other objects cannot.

TO PROVE TO SOMEONE THAT YOU STILL HAVE IT. This may be a book that you are otherwise ready to give away, but because a friend gifted it, you want to make sure you have it on display when they visit. This I've found happens a lot with coffee table books. It can be a little frustrating when the biggest books are the ones you want to get rid of the most, yet, you are beholden to keeping them. This dilemma is probably better suited to "Dear Abby" than to our guidance here. You will know if it's time to part ways with a book if you notice it frequently and agonize over the need to keep it to stay friends with the person who gifted it. You should probably donate it to a good organization and then tell your friend you spilled coffee all over it and had to recycle it!

TO MAKE YOUR SHELVES LOOK GOOD. There is no shame in keeping books just because they look good. It's great if your books all belong on your shelves for multiple reasons, but if it's only one reason and that reason is that it looks good, that is good enough for us. When you need room for new acquisitions, maybe cull some books that only look good and aren't serving other purposes.

What if you are in a family household and not the only one making decisions about what stays and what goes?

Here are a few scenarios you might come across as you cull your books:

"I loved this story at one time and could give it away, but what about the kids? I should keep it. Maybe they will read it and love it like I did!"

"I haven't gone to a yoga class in years, let alone looked at these yoga books. But my partner has talked about going to a class recently. Maybe I should keep these books just in case."

"These are my partner's books but I hate how they look and how they remind me of her life before we got together. My books are so much nicer!"

"I know this book doesn't serve any purpose for me now. But what if it does later and I regret giving it away? It will be wasteful if I just have to purchase the book again. I should keep it."

"These are my kids' books. They think they are baby books now, but will they want them when they grow up as a way to reconnect with their childhood?"

SCOTT JUREK EAT RUN

Matt Fitzgerald · The NEW RULES of MARATHON and HALF-MARATHON NUTRITION · A CUTTING-EDGE PLAN TO FUEL YOUR BODY BEYOND "THE WALL"

Matt Fitzgerald · 80/20 RUNNING · RUN STRONGER AND RACE FASTER BY TRAINING SLOWER

RUN · THE MIND-BODY METHOD OF RUNNING BY FEEL · Fitzgerald

HEART RATE TRAINING · BENSON · CONNOLLY

RUNNING THE LYDIARD WAY · By Arthur Lydiard with Garth Gilmour

MORE FIRE · How to Run the Kenyan Way · Toby Tanser

RUNNING with Lydiard · Lydiard/Gilmour

The scenarios on the previous page reflect potentially valid reasons to keep books or at least have family discussions about whether books stay or go. Every family and household dynamic is different.

Perhaps you can initiate a discussion with your family about the books. You may find a resounding answer as to whether your kids or partner wants you to keep a certain book.

Or maybe you should just do the work and be decisive. Cull the shelves and put some boxes in the garage for a few months to see if anyone misses their books. If you get a question about where someone's favorite book went, you can bring it back and then talk about donating the rest.

You can also create a limbo area to store the "maybe someday" books and mark them with a note: "To be given away on [date]. Take what you want before then, otherwise they will be gone!"

When reviewing existing client libraries, Thatcher has found a common trend:

the binge purchase. The collection of books that reflect a *very* distinct time: that day you discovered a certain parenting expert or the keto diet and bought all the books you could find on Amazon. You may still be into these subjects, but you don't need an entire collection of them. Keep one title that serves as the best reflection or touchpoint and part with the rest.

Like the cards in a card catalog, one book can serve as a symbolic sign of the whole. (The photo above is a part of Elizabeth's "wanting to be a faster runner" story.) She has since realized she's not a fast runner, and so now has just one title to remind her it's still a good practice to want to improve.

For your rare books, or titles with value, seek out a trusted rare book dealer or auction house. They can help you discern which books have value and share with you the appropriate next steps.

There are countless ways to help your books find new life in another's home. Here are a few ideas:

📚 **HOST AN ESTATE OR YARD SALE.** Price the books to sell—usually around one or two dollars per book.

📚 **TRADE IN GENTLY-USED BOOKS TO YOUR LOCAL BOOKSTORE.** Usually you will receive credit toward a new purchase. If they accept twenty of your books and give you enough credit to buy one beautiful coffee table book that you love, consider it a victory!

📚 **SELL YOUR BOOKS ONLINE.** Amazon or eBay are the most accessible to work with for individuals. Abebooks.com is also a great site to look up values on rare books and first editions. Be patient with online sales. There can be a lot of competition but if you have books in nice condition, they should sell if priced right.

📚 **GIVE AWAY BOOKS TO YOUR LOCAL LIBRARY.** They will sell them to raise money at their next library sale (which is also a great place to shop for more books, by the way!). This is usually the easiest way to part with a lot of books.

📚 **GIVE BOOKS TO NONPROFITS OR SCHOOLS.** They will let you know if they need books for their shelves or if they can sell them in their thrift store, upcoming book or yard sale, or in another way to raise money for a cause you support.

📚 **RESPONSIBLY RECYCLE YOUR BOOKS.** This may take a little more work to figure out who recycles books, but if the books will never sell (perhaps due to damage), it's far better to recycle them than for them to end up in a landfill.

📚 **CONSTRUCT A LITTLE FREE LIBRARY** on your property or add your books to one in your neighborhood.

📚 **SOME PLACES LIKE DOCTORS' WAITING ROOMS,** nursing homes, and preschools accept donations of age-appropriate books.

📚 **CHECK OUT BOOKCROSSING.COM** and create a game and sense of community around clearing your books.

"We don't need to have just one favorite. We keep adding favorites. Our favorite book is always the book that speaks most directly to us at a particular stage in our lives. And our lives change. We have other favorites that give us what we most need at that particular time. But we never lose the old favorites. They're always with us. We just sort of accumulate them."

—Lloyd Alexander[2]

With every book purge can come a season of book mourning when you realize you gave a book away too soon. The great thing about books is that you can usually find another copy. One way in which the internet serves us is that most used and rare book dealers publish their catalogs online. However, there may be a few that you part with that are irreplaceable.

In the early days of his bookselling years, Thatcher kept a lot more books for his personal collection than he does now. Having been in the trade for more than seventeen years, he knows what he is likely to see again and which books he shouldn't miss an opportunity to acquire. Books are fluid; they should come and go like a river flowing in and out of your life, enriching and serving as signposts to tell your story.

Preparing to Rearrange
Your Books or
to Start a New Library

REARRANGING YOUR SHELVES can be a lot of work but it doesn't have to be overwhelming. It's a good idea to prepare for the task and know exactly what you are getting yourself into. The results are definitely worth it, but, like anything else, you want to make sure that you are ready so that once you start the project you can see it through with minimal stress.

Once you've decided to rearrange your books, here's where to start:

MENTALLY PREPARE: Set aside a few days or weeks for this project. You don't want to feel too stressed or physically taxed from the experience.

PHYSICALLY PREPARE: Make sure you have all the materials you need on hand (see pages 220–221 for a list) so that you can sort and reach things with ease.

ASK FOR HELP: Hire a professional, or ask a friend to have a glass of wine with you, while you work through the shelves. The process is much easier with another set of hands and it helps to have someone with whom to discuss what looks good and your connections to various books.

ADJUST SHELF HEIGHTS: Adjusting the shelf height is much easier to do when the shelves are empty. Cull some of your books so that you're working with less weight on the shelves.

THOUGHTFULLY DISCARD: Sell books or give away those that no longer belong in your collection. See our tips on page 212 for donating or trading in your books.

CATALOG YOUR BOOKS: A basic spreadsheet program is really all you need to make a list of your books, however there are programs and apps that will help you take the cataloging to a new level.

Cleaning Books

Books are durable and last a long time, but over the years they can pick up dirt and benefit from a cleaning.

The first step in cleaning a book is to determine what materials you are trying to clean. Many of the materials that go into books don't respond well to liquids and you want to be careful with old or rare books.

Glossy modern jackets are the easiest part of a modern book to clean. We recommend rubbing alcohol (70 percent) to take off any marks and give them a general refreshing. Note that some jackets are laminated on both sides, while others are only laminated on one side. Be careful with any moisture applied to paper with a non-glossy finish as the jacket could be damaged in the cleaning process.

Paper and cloth bindings require a little more of a delicate approach as they may not be able to tolerate any contact with moisture. We recommend using only a damp cloth or the following techniques and tools.

A Staedtler white eraser is an indispensable tool around our office. You can use the eraser to clean up marks on the jackets or in the books (pencil notes, used book prices, etc.), you can also use it to rub away adhesive residue from stickers. If there are smudge marks on the page edges of a book, you can also clean them up with the eraser. Rub firmly, then blow away the eraser fragments. The Staedtler white eraser is also phenomenally effective at rubbing away marks and stains on cloth and paper bindings. It won't take away that coffee ring but it will clean up any superficial discolorations.

The top edge of books can get dusty over the years. We use either a microfiber cloth to wipe the dust free, or a Swiffer dusting cloth. Some people like those compressed

Part Three

air cans to blow away dust, but it will just send the dust somewhere else and land on your books eventually! There are also mini-vacuums that professional librarians use to clean lots of books at a time, some with attachments that allow you to clean books without removing them from the shelves.

For more advanced cleaning such as removing old bookplates or more troublesome adhesives under stickers, we typically first try to use a palette knife with a smooth edge (available from your local art supply store). Try to get under one of the corners and then delicately peel the bookplate off. Depending on the age of the bookplate and the type of adhesive used, it may come off easily. If not, you might need to make a decision about whether the book looks better keeping the bookplate or sticker in place, or possibly putting a new one of the same size over it. If you proceed with the removal, there is a risk that the book will show permanent damage in that place, however you can use rubber cement as a tool for one adhesive to attract and remove another adhesive. Or a hair dryer works wonders to essentially "fry and dry" the adhesive; then remove the bookplate or sticker little by little.

Moisture damage is a trickier issue to address. If your books are heavily damaged by flooding or exposure to water, one tip is to put them in plastic bags and into the freezer as quickly as possible while you make a plan and consult an expert on whether the books can be salvaged. The freezer is also a good place to arrest any insect damage to books.

If you end up with a book with an unpleasant odor (e.g., smoke or mildew) after returning from a used book buying spree, one strategy to see if it can be improved is to place the book in an airtight plastic bag with a few dryer sheets to draw the odor out. Three days usually works. Then you can dispose of the bag and dryer sheets. The freezer trick is also worth trying to eliminate odors in the books you really want to keep.

Elizabeth, historically, had always been the type of reader who would simply place her books as they arrived straight on the shelf, with no organizational direction or thought beyond where they would fit. She has a good memory so she was able to get by this way for decades, but eventually the haphazard system broke down. Books were stacked double-rowed within the bookshelves and piled on the floor, and her memory of where she'd placed one title over another could no longer keep up. Chaos reigned. Does this sound familiar?

Needing to find relief and to not feel burdened or overwhelmed by the books she owned and loved, Elizabeth dove into the hard work of organizing—first by taking everything off of the bookcases, clearing out the clutter, and then, lastly, putting the books back on the shelf.

In her words:

After living with my bookshelves for years without much notice, I walked into the living room one day and was confronted by them with fresh eyes. My bookshelves were bursting

with books! Double-rowed and stacked, each spine was fighting for place on the shelf.

Just by being on the shelf, each book did indeed reveal a piece of me—my character, my interests, glimpses into who I was and what I found important. Yet the organization (or lack thereof) revealed a piece of me, too—one that I was eager to shift. Each book belonged in my story. I just needed a way to tell the story better.

I had seen quite a few images on Pinterest with books organized by color and the effect was stunning. So when I first began to organize my shelves, I tried it out! The look was indeed striking. I loved it.

Over the course of several months, I started shifting books—moving one here, another there—and much to my surprise, the arrangement that worked best emerged, almost as if by magic. The books themselves seemed to sort out where they wanted to be.

I discovered that I tend to like books by one author grouped together and from there loosely arranged by color (unless I get the sense that one book really needs to be by a particular book, like an energy-pull). The kids' and art books are on the lower shelves. There's also a section for new books that can rest there until they are added to the to-be-read pile by my bed or placed in their rightful spot on the shelves.

It's intuitive, not rigid. It has its own sense of organization that my family and I understand, yet has enough wiggle room to simply haphazardly pop a book on the shelf when need be.

The takeaway? There is some work involved in your commitment to rearranging or redoing your bookshelves. If you are lucky enough to start with an empty bookcase or library, you can fill it with intention in a stylish manner.

Preparing to Rearrange Your Books or to Start a New Library

ANNE
OF AVONLEA

ANNE OF
THE ISLAND

ANNE'S
HOUSE OF
DREAMS

RILLA OF
INGLESIDE

RAINBOW
VALLEY

Nearly Infinite Ways to Arrange the Same Books

NOW WE'RE READY! Here is the nitty-gritty on exactly how to style your bookcases. With a few tools and a little time, your dream library is within reach.

On the following pages you'll find a list of ideas to consider when doing the work of rearranging your books. Then in the next chapter, there are specific steps to follow when styling your bookshelves. There is no one correct way to place your books on your shelves, so hopefully you enjoy trying out these concepts until you find what works for you!

As you experiment and try different systems, you will see how the story you are telling shifts with different placements of the books. Trust the process and the story you were meant to tell.

Big Decisions

There are a few decisions to make about how to arrange your books that are good to settle on *before* you start shelving your books. For example, whether to arrange your books:

ALPHABETICALLY BY AUTHOR. For most literary collections, it's nice to organize the books alphabetically by author so you know where to find Jane Austen or Zadie Smith. For nonfiction and other subjects, this method may not be as good of a fit.

ALPHABETICALLY OR CHRONOLOGICALLY BY TITLE OR SUBJECT. For histories, biographies, and other nonfiction, it probably makes more sense to order these by topic. For example, when Thatcher installs a collection of US presidential biographies, he tries to do so chronologically in order of the presidential terms.

BY SUBJECT. A traditional library organizational plan would be to keep like subjects together so that you can go around the room and say "There's poetry, there's classic literature, there are my histories," and so on.

BY COLOR—ROYGBIV. This sounds superficial but it looks really cool to make a rainbow with your books. The books are yours; don't let anyone tell you this is a silly idea. A lot of people remember the color of their favorite books, so when someone asks you how you will ever find that Samantha Bee book you love, just tell them, "It's easy. It's pink and I know exactly where it is!"

BY COLOR—LIGHT TO DARK OR OTHER COLOR PLAN. Thatcher tends to think of bookshelves as being a canvas that goes from big and dark on the bottom to small and light on the top. This doesn't always work out exactly, but as an operating principle, it offers a way to ground bookshelves with the darker, bigger books on the bottom.

BY SIZE ON THE SHELVES. Placing larger books closer to the floor is grounding and it makes them more accessible as well. You can still place horizontal stacks of big books on the upper shelves, though. We are all for that variety.

BY CHRONOLOGICAL ORDER OF PUBLICATION.
For the works of one author, it often makes sense to arrange the books in chronological order of publication. For Ernest Hemingway, you'd start with *In Our Time* and end with either *The Old Man and the Sea* or one of his posthumously published works. With subjects that are important to you, you may arrange them this way, such as a collection of Civil War books beginning with those published during or just after the war, leading up to more modern, scholarly works. This can be a nice way to show off the depth and breadth of your collection.

BY CHRONOLOGICAL ORDER OF ACQUISI-TION DATE. Another way to arrange books is based on when they came into your life. This approach tells more of your story: where you were and who you were at particular points in your life.

BY PUBLISHER. Some publishers have really strong brands and are known for publishing certain types of books. Organizing your books by publisher is related to organizing books by subject if there is a really recognizable theme throughout their work.

Considerations for How All the Books Should Look as a Whole

BOOKS OF SIMILAR FORMAT OR BINDING:
Grouped together or spread apart? For
example, dividing paperbacks and hardcovers, separating art and oversize books
from novels, or grouping all leather-bound
books together. Generally, we are believers
in weaving an interesting story through the
shelves and having one's eye discover new
things over time. Finding a binding that is
different than others is something fun to
discover. Having a group of books in one
specific binding might stand out too much,

creating a distraction from the rest of the
library.

KEEP JACKETS ON OR REMOVE THEM?
For collectible books and first editions,
the book jacket represents a substantial
portion of the value of the book, so we
wouldn't recommend removing those jackets unless you have a secure place to store
them, should you choose to sell the books
later. For all other books, some people
prefer the look of books without modern

jackets—the jackets tend to be glossy and reflect glare, the colors more intense. Removing them creates a more muted palette. It is a personal preference and completely up to you and your style.

PLACING CERTAIN BOOKS AT EYE LEVEL. If you leave the room and then come back in, where does your eye go on the shelves first? When you are standing in front of the bookcases, which shelves are you looking at? We would argue that you should pay the most attention to these shelves and what is on them. Curate these selections to perfection as you and your guests will see them more than anything else.

PLACING CERTAIN BOOKS WITHIN REACH OR OUT OF REACH. You may want to bring some intentionality to which books are low to the ground, in reach of the kids. You should also think about which books are shelved up high and made less visible. You know the books we're talking about!

Considerations Within Each Shelf

BY SIZE ON EACH SHELF. On each shelf you have a choice how to place the books. For example either with big books in the center and smaller books at the edges, or from small to big, from left to right, or right to left.

VERTICAL VS. HORIZONTAL. You also can decide on whether to have all the books standing straight up or all stacked horizontally, or a mix of the two. We like to have about half the shelf full of books standing straight up, then anchor them with a small horizontal stack that brings the fill rate of the shelves up to about ⅔ full.

GROUPING BOOKS IN EVEN OR ODD NUMBERS. Thatcher will confess to some OCD when it comes to arranging books and he definitely has a preference for these numbers of books grouped together: three, five, eight, ten, etc.

Other people like even numbers of books. If this matters to you, then it's important. If not, focus on other considerations!

STRATEGICALLY LEANING BOOKS. This can be applied to make the shelves more organic and playful. Note that books will warp if you leave them leaning for a long time.

SYMMETRY VERSUS ASYMMETRY. Some people can only live with a symmetrical arrangement, often down to the number of books on a shelf and having the mirror image of an arrangement on each side of a room. Others love to make the shelves dance with variations that create unique arrangements as your eye scans the shelves. Thatcher likes to create asymmetrical arrangements, but then repeat them for some symmetry around the room.

THE FRONT OF THE SHELF VERSUS THE BACK OF THE SHELF. There are two types of people in this world: those who place their books at the front of the shelf and those who put them in the back. Thatcher is definitely a front-of-the-shelf person. Every installation he works on, the books are within about ¾ of an inch of the front of the shelf. However, others love to push their books to the back, often placing objects (Funko Pop, anyone?) in front of their books. The back-of-the-shelf crowd argues that it's also easier to dust the shelves with the books at the back. A combination of front and back of the shelves can also be applied to strategically place and layer objects. It can be very to fun to make the shelves more three-dimensional with objects and books at different depths, if it works for you.

HOW FULL SHOULD YOUR SHELVES BE? If you have too many books and not enough shelves, or you prefer the regularity of every book standing straight up, go for 100 percent full. If you like a more balanced look with variation and room for growth, the rule of thirds can be very magical—67 percent full with books and 33 percent with accessories. If you are going for modern and minimalist, perhaps with a lot of horizontal stacks, go for anywhere from 25 percent to 50 percent full with books.

FACE OUT BOOKS. There are a lot of individual books with gorgeous covers, why not show them off by placing the book with its front cover facing out? Book covers are artwork after all.

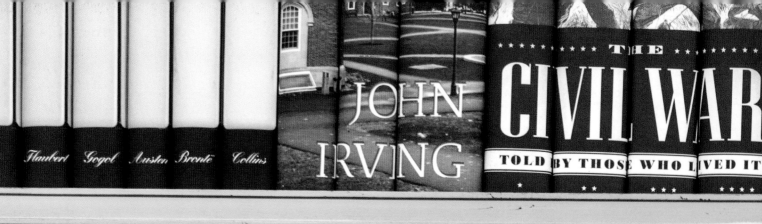

Eco   Flaubert   Gogol   Austen   Brontë   Collins

JOHN IRVING

THE CIVIL WAR
TOLD BY THOSE WHO LIVED IT

THE WORKS OF WILLIAM FAULKNER

The Town, The Mansion, The Reivers

THE HANDMAID'S TALE
ATWOOD

OLD GORIOT
BALZAC

JANE EYRE
BRONTË

THE PLAGUE, THE FALL, EXILE AND THE KINGDOM
CAMUS

THE DIV

THE ODYSSEY
HOMER

THE ILIAD
HOMER

THE BOOKSHOP, THE GATE OF ANGELS, THE BLUE FLOWER
FITZGERALD

GOLF

SKIING

TENNIS

YACHTING

EQUESTRIAN

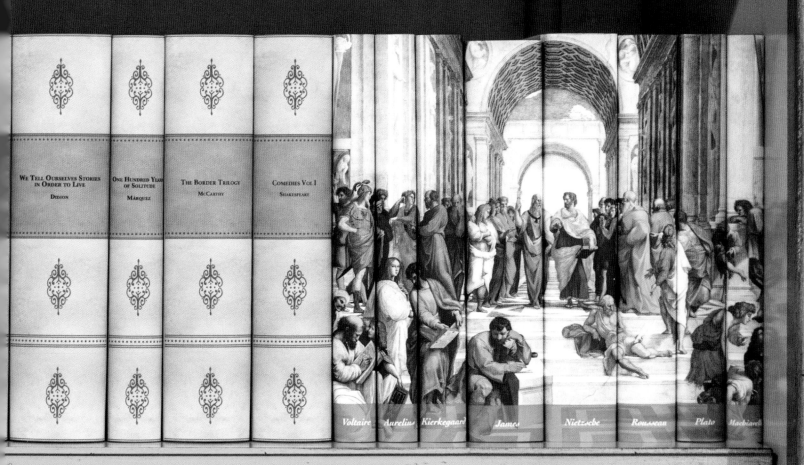

We Tell Ourselves Stories in Order to Live — DIDION

One Hundred Years of Solitude — MÁRQUEZ

The Border Trilogy — MCCARTHY

Comedies Vol. I — SHAKESPEARE

Voltaire Aurelius Kierkegaard James Nietzsche Rousseau Plato Machiavelli

LIVING IN STYLE SCANDINAVIA — teNeues

LIVING IN STYLE MOUNTAIN CHALETS — teNeues

LIVING IN STYLE COUNTRY — teNeues

Ernest Hemingway — DEATH IN THE AFTERNOON — SCRIBNER CLASSICS

Ernest Hemingway — A FAREWELL TO ARMS — SCRIBNER CLASSICS

ALBUQUERQUE — ANAYA

OUT OF AFRICA — ISAK DINESEN

E. L. DOCTOROW — RAGTIME — MODERN LIBRARY

THE YEARLING — Marjorie Kinnan Rawlings — SCRIBNERS

GEORGE ELIOT — THE MILL ON THE FLOSS — EVERYMAN'S LIBRARY

JANE AUSTEN — EMMA — EVERYMAN'S LIBRARY

CHARLOTTE BRONTË — VILLETTE — EVERYMAN'S LIBRARY

John Updike — HUGGING THE SHORE — Alfred A. Knopf

CHANDLER — Stories & Early Novels

MARK TWAIN — Mississippi Writings

THE EGYPTIANS — ALAN GARDINER — FOLIO SOCIETY

THE HITTITES — O. M. GURNEY — FOLIO SOCIETY

THE PERSIANS — J. M. COOK — FOLIO SOCIETY

John Updike — SELF-CONSCIOUSNESS — Alfred A. Knopf

KURT VONNEGUT — DEADEYE DICK — DELACORTE PRESS / LAWRENCE

Kurt Vonnegut — BAGOMBO SNUFF BOX — Putnam

The Heart is a Lonely Hunter — McCULLERS — H. M. CO.

THE COLLECTED AUTOBIOGRAPHIES of MAYA ANGELOU — INCLUDES I Know Why the Caged Bird Sings

GEORGE ELIOT — DANIEL DERONDA — EVERYMAN'S LIBRARY

ANNE BRONTË — AGNES GREY / THE TENANT OF WILDFELL HALL — EVERYMAN'S LIBRARY

HOMAGE TO CATALONIA — DOWN AND OUT IN PARIS AND LONDON — GEORGE ORWELL — HMH

THE COLOR PURPLE — THE TEMPLE OF MY FAMILIAR — ALICE WALKER — HMH

Step-by-Step: How to Style a Bookcase

Step One: Before

LOOK AT YOUR SHELVES as they are and perhaps take a picture for reference's sake. As we did in the living room, do a quick scan of the size, color, and subject of each book. Take note of the actual shelves, their height and depth, the width, and how the shelves are grouped. Then think about the purpose of the room.

Step Two: Remove books from shelves

Next, take everything off the shelf so you are working with a blank slate. Give yourself this gift of a fresh start. Now that your books are gathered, start to organize them by subject—this helps to create a visual map of the books you have.

As you start to sort by genre—art, architecture, and travel for instance—you can then easily discern how much space is needed and their positioning, whether they should be stacked vertically spine to spine, placed in horizontal stacks, or perhaps a combination of both.

STEP THREE: PLACE OBJECTS AND TEST BOOKS' POSITIONS

Slowly put the books back, playing with how they are arranged. This is the time to experiment a bit, find visual patterns

by mixing spine colors, or playing with subject-oriented shelves to find the best movement. This eye toward fluidity makes the books more visually pleasing, inviting the viewer to follow a linear flow and discover new books while feeling relaxed in the space. Play with placing objects on the shelves surrounding your books, offering yet another piece to the story.

This first phase is really a time to experiment, nothing is written in stone. It's a time to play and find which modes of organization are most appealing to you and work best for your space.

STEP FOUR: MOVE BOOKS (EVEN IF YOU LOVE THEM) IF THEY DON'T LOOK RIGHT

Sometimes a book you love goes on the shelf and it dominates the entire look. Don't

worry, the book doesn't need to go, it just needs to go somewhere else. Elizabeth had a hardcover copy of *Roald Dahl's Book of Ghost Stories* at the end of a shelf, and the front cover is a rather creepy large-scale photo of the author. Every time Elizabeth would walk in the living room, all she would see was Roald Dahl staring back at her. So she moved the book to the middle of a shelf, spine out. Problem solved. The spine was pretty benign and blended in beautifully with other books.

STEP FIVE: TEST OUT VERTICAL AND HORIZONTAL PLACEMENTS

Experimenting with a variety of horizontal and vertical book stackings instantly breathes life and movement into the shelves and also serves as an easy way to highlight

objects within the mix, while still using the maximum amount of space. It's also a great solution for taller books that you would still like to feature on standard-sized shelves.

STEP SIX: EXPERIMENTING WITH DIFFERENT TYPES OF OBJECTS AND ACCESSORIES

You've played a bit with objects in Step Three, and probably have an idea of which ones enhance the story of your books. As you inch toward a completed shelf, consider the placement of these accessories. Stack books as a horizontal support for your objects or use one to prop your books into position. Be careful that the books aren't too heavy and won't push the object over, causing something beloved to fall and break.

STEP SEVEN: EXPERIMENT WITH PLACING PRETTY COVERS WITH FRONT FACING OUT

Placing books with attractive front covers with their front facing out brings an element of surprise to the shelf. Booksellers often do this with new releases to draw a customer's attention, and there is no reason to not bring this tip home! Sometimes Thatcher places front facing books at the back of the bookcase so they are resting against the wall and other times, if the book is nice and solid, it can be placed at the front. Play with the depth and see what you prefer. Overall, we prefer all the books at the front edge of

try multiple systems within your shelves. Group similar authors together and then continue to fill the space with similar subject matter, or see if your eye feels more relaxed sorting by color. Maybe you separate fiction and nonfiction, or find that they go better mixed together by subject matter—your Martin Walker mysteries fitting perfectly beside Peter Mayle's musings on Provence. The options are endless and entirely personal.

STEP NINE: TRY MORE UNUSUAL OBJECTS

An old phone, a crystal . . . anything might work. Perhaps you have an antique clock that can go on your shelf beside your beloved copy of *A Wrinkle in Time* or a seated Buddha statue next to your copy of Jack Kerouac's *The Dharma Bums*.

the bookcase—maybe half an inch from the front—but again, it is simply a preference.

STEP EIGHT: FIND THEMES TO REPEAT

Authors, images, subjects, colors. . . . As we mentioned above, there are myriad ways to organize your books and you can

STEP TEN: FINE TUNE

See if some books look better without their jackets; you can always store the jacket separately and reunite it with the book at a later date. With rare books, the original dust jacket is often a key part of the value, and so sometimes it is a good idea to take the jacket off and store it safely, while also making sense from a design standpoint for your space.

STEP ELEVEN: TRUST YOUR GUT

Sometimes mixing antique and modern works well, sometimes it doesn't. The minute the right book goes in the wrong spot, you will feel the shift instantly. Just set that book aside, another spot will appear as you continue to style the shelves.

STEP TWELVE: TAKE A STEP BACK

As you work, continue to step back to perceive the whole. Sometimes things that seem to work up close don't work so well from a distance. To save some time and avoid having to change entire shelves, keep stepping back to gain perspective.

STEP THIRTEEN: GROUP BOOKS BY COLOR SUBJECT AND SIZE

Play with shades of color and try interspersing a different tone between two similar shades to break up the continuity and provide a surprise for the eye. Color coding that isn't too spot-on is often an elegant approach.

STEP FOURTEEN: BE PATIENT
WITH THE PROCESS

Sometimes it takes a while, and different combinations, for the shelves to start to feel right.

When you find the right mix, the shelves will have character that reflect who you are and they will really feel like they belong in your home.

Reading the Books You Have

WE WROTE THIS BOOK because we believe passionately in the power of books. Books to read and tell us stories, books to surround us and to tell our story to the world (and ourselves).

So here's the part where we tell you to go and read your books!

Reading has tremendous benefits, especially in the digitally overloaded, time-starved world we live in. Books can help reduce our stress level. Reading printed books helps our brains retain more information. Reading in general increases empathy and books quite simply can bring us a lot of joy!

"What a miracle it is that out of these small, flat, rigid squares of paper unfolds world after world after world, worlds that sing to you, comfort and quiet or excite you. Books help us understand who we are and how we are to behave. They show us what community and friendship mean; they show us how to live and die."

—Anne Lamott

This book hopefully inspires you to overhaul your shelves. That's great. But please also make time to read your books or at least hold them close and remember why you have them, who you are, and who you want to be.

It is so tempting to pick up our phones and tablets, scroll through our social media feeds, turn on the TV, or watch a show on our laptops. We would suggest that we also make time for books and reading—to find some balance between looking at screens all day—and holding a printed book in your hands.

Technology can be used in positive ways to develop good reading habits. You can set a daily reminder on your phone for dedicated reading time. You can use a laptop to catalog your library, and keep a list in the cloud for your whole family to reference when they go looking for a book. You can be inspired by great films based on books to then go and read the book. You can find just about any book ever printed online from sellers around the world alongside an ever-expanding list of print-on-demand titles.

Loving good, old-fashioned printed books is not about being a Luddite; you can love books and still buy and love the latest iPhone. Instead of resisting modern technology and the way the modern world works, harness what's new to give your life more balance.

Tips to find more time to read in an age when it feels as if there is no time.

WAKE UP A LITTLE EARLIER. Make reading part of your morning ritual.

TAKE A BOOK WITH YOU WHEREVER YOU GO. There are always ten or fifteen minutes of time throughout the day to read a chapter. This will also help with small bits of digital detox, turning to a book rather than your phone.

TRACK YOUR TIME. Elizabeth once read an article that suggested she may have more free time than she'd thought and to find this time, track it. For three days, she tracked how she spent her time, writing down where even the smallest moments went. Through this process, she found pockets of time scrolling through social media or distractedly browsing websites. Once she noticed these moments, she started choosing a book instead—whether for five minutes or ten minutes, each page adds up and creates a more delightful and intentional day.

SLOW DOWN. The world is moving at a faster and faster pace and it shows no sign of slowing down. But we can choose to slow down and be present in every moment. Books help us slow down, sit in one place, and immerse ourselves in the now as we comprehend and absorb what we are reading.

EMBRACE AN AUDIOBOOK SUBSCRIPTION. While this is not reading, per se, audiobooks are a great way to immerse yourself in stories when it is inconvenient or impossible to read, such as during a morning commute or while exercising. Thatcher loves audiobooks and they now account for about 40 percent of his book consumption. It started on long drives when he was a kid—popping audio cassettes into the car stereo—and has evolved with Audible on his phone, consumed mostly at bedtime. Audiobooks are also available at public libraries (often on disk or by digital download).

DIGITAL DETOX. Consider having a dedicated time of day—or week, month, or year—where you do not use your devices and instead focus on being fully

present in conversations, your work, your art or writing, your thoughts, and what you are reading. You don't have to swear off all devices forever, just find the balance. Notice if there are benefits for you and then cultivate a sustainable schedule for getting done what you need to do and being happy.

MAKE A DEDICATED SPACE FOR READING. This book has lots of ideas for arranging books in your home. Outside the house, you might have a place, or lists of places, you regularly read—the local library, a park, a coffee shop, or even public transit.

If we all read more books, the world would be a much better place.

It all can start with one book. One person. One home. It's in your hands now.

Happy reading,
Thatcher & Elizabeth

> "That is the inimitable power of literature, to give context and meaning to the trials and triumphs of living."
>
> —Charles M. Blow[1]

Part Three

"You think your pain and your heartbreak are unprecedented in the history of the world, but then you read. It was Dostoevsky and Dickens who taught me that the things that tormented me the most were the very things that connected me with all the people who were alive, who had ever been alive."

—James Baldwin

Acknowledgments

THE CONCEPT FOR taking what Juniper Books does and putting it into the beautiful book you hold in your hands had been an idea for a long time. However, as a busy entrepreneur and dad, I never had the time to sit down and start writing. Then in 2017, I was forced to slow down when I went through cancer treatment for lymphoma. On many of the days when I was too weak and ill to get to the office, I stayed home and wrote. I made a resolution during this time that when I emerged from cancer and chemotherapy, I wouldn't just sell other people's books; I was going to write some of my own. In the spring of 2018, just as I was getting back to work full-time, an email came in from Katie Killebrew at Gibbs Smith. Would I like to collaborate "on a home library book—part inspirational, part instructional?" Gibbs Smith wanted to publish such a book and as luck would have it, I had already started writing that book.

Thank you to the entire team at Gibbs Smith including Katie Killebrew, Shelby Kisgen, and Michelle Branson for seeing this book through from idea to reality. Thank you for believing in me, in Juniper Books, and for getting behind this creation 100 percent.

Before committing to writing the book, I asked my friend, long-time customer, and business advisor Elizabeth Lane to coauthor the book with me. I knew I couldn't finish the book on my own; I was susceptible to getting too busy all over again! Thank you, Elizabeth, for keeping me on schedule, for bringing your love of books to every aspect of the production, and for all of your support and trust in Juniper Books.

Thank you to Jordan Singer, our longtime photographer at Juniper Books, for organizing and shooting such a great archive of our work over the years—many images from that archive appear on these pages. Thank you to Samantha Hahn for contributing such a fresh and beautiful perspective to this publication through your illustrations.

For the Love of Books reflects nearly two decades of collaborations with thousands of clients, helping them tell their stories through the books on their shelves. Juniper Books has too many clients to list and thank them all here, however I am truly grateful to every single person who has ever purchased a book, a set, or a complete library from Juniper Books.

An extra special thank you to all the clients who allowed us to photograph their bookshelves and their homes. For privacy reasons, we have not included your names but please know how grateful I am for allowing us this privilege.

Over the years we have had the pleasure of getting to know and work with some of the world's top interior designers, architects, builders, visual merchandisers, and other design trade professionals. Many of our collaborations are reflected on these pages. Thank you for trusting us to elevate books and libraries together.

Thank you to all of the press and media who have written about us. You recognized that what we were doing was different and unusual in the digital era. I appreciate the space and time you dedicated to tell our story and truly believe we have contributed to the marvelous comeback of the printed book in recent years.

Dozens of team members have contributed to the creativity, attention to detail, and success of Juniper Books over the eighteen years we have been in business. I'd especially like to thank Sandra Greenway, Kirsten Herzig, Jenn Hyde, and Kaitlin Gilland for all of their hard work, their love of books, and their dedication to making our customers happy.

For the philosophy that appears on these pages, it could have remained in my head much longer had it not been for Virginia Santy, who helped me with my TED Talk in 2016 ("The Books We Keep, the Stories We Tell") and with getting my ideas down on paper.

Back in 2001, when I was leaving the tech world, I followed my good friend Ryan McMillen around as he bought and sold books in New England. Ryan first showed me how to research rare books and tell their stories. I have gone in a lot of different directions since then, but it all comes back to books and the stories they tell. For that initial spark, I am very grateful.

From an early age, my parents showed me that anything is possible; there is no such thing as a bad idea, and that if some people think what you are doing is crazy, you just might be on to something. They owned and operated a legendary restaurant in New York City in the 1980s called The Quilted Giraffe. They took a concept (running a restaurant) that had been around a long time and reinvented every aspect of it. I'd like to think that I'm carrying on their legacy, but with books instead of food. My mother, Susan Wine, came to work for Juniper Books at a critical time in the company's history, helping us to grow the business and for that I am very appreciative. My father, Barry Wine, has always been one of my biggest supporters and confidantes. I am extremely grateful for his creativity and counsel, and also for the amazing meals he cooks on my visits to New York.

—Thatcher Wine

First, a huge thank you to Thatcher Wine for inviting me to coauthor this book with him. A kindred spirit in all things books, this was an absolute delight to write (and it inspired me to look at my own bookshelves with a more discerning eye)!

To the most talented person I know, Samantha Hahn, my creative director at Quarterlane (QL), and true guide and friend for the past three years. I discovered your artwork in a stunning book by a mutual friend and working with you since has been the greatest gift. To have your illustrations in *For the Love of Books* brings me more joy than you could ever know. The most talented artist, the most indomitable person, you are an inspiration. Thank you for your friendship, dedication, and support through QL and beyond.

To Courtney Peterson Lindsey for helping me in the early stages of QL. Without your steadfast support, books in beautiful boxes would have remained a dream.

To my Quarterlane dream team of photographers: Christine Han, Nicki Sebastian, Nick Steever, Kimberly Murray, Michelle Drewes, Christine Lane, and Danlly Domingo. You first brought your magic to *The QL Edit* and *The QL Kids Magazine,* showcasing books and the people that love them. I'm incredibly honored to bring that magic to these pages. Thank you so very much.

Thank you, also, to the booklovers who shared their homes and their stories with me. I am so very grateful.

To Lydia Gollner and everyone with whom I work at Partners Village Store, my home away from home in Westport, Massachusetts. It's a joy to go to work every day and I'm thankful to you all!

To my family, who supported QL from the beginning, and now have homes piled with fiction. Mom and Dad, Katherine Reay, Ross Blackburn, Sarah Kay, Rachel Towne, Meg Whalen, and Sally Soter—I love you and thank you for your unwavering support.

Finally, thank you to Gardner, Edie, and Emily, whom I love the most, even more than books.

—*Elizabeth Lane*

Notes

THE BOOKS WE KEEP, THE STORIES WE TELL

1 Didion, Joan, *The White Album: Essays* (New York: FSG Classics, 2009).

2 Childress, Diana, *Johannes Gutenberg and the Printing Press* (Minneapolis: Twenty-First Century Books, 2007), 44.

3 Mikanowski, Jacob, "A Secret Library, Digitally Excavated," *New Yorker* (October 9, 2013).

4 Houston, Keith, *The Book* (New York: W. W. Norton & Company, 2016), 250.

5 Houston, *The Book,* 251.

6 Man, John, *The Gutenberg Revolution: How Printing Changed the Course of History* (London: Transworld Publishers, 2010), 16.

7 Kurlansky, Mark, *Paper: Paging Through History* (New York: W. W. Norton & Company, 2017), 116–117.

THE RESILIENCE OF THE PRINTED BOOK IN THE DIGITAL ERA

1 Rabinowitz, Paula, *American Pulp* (Princeton University Press, 2014), 3.

2 Rabinowitz, *American Pulp,* 3.

3 Mendand, Louis, "Pulp's Big Moment," *New Yorker* (January 5, 2015). https://www.newyorker.com/magazine/2015/01/05/pulps-big-moment?

4 Mendand, "Pulp's Big Moment."

5 Rabinowitz, *American Pulp,* 256–257.

BOOKS IN OUR HOMES— HOW DID THEY GET THERE?

1 "The ALA 10 most challenged books in 2017." https://www.bookbub.com/blog/2018/04/10/ala—most—challenged—books—2017

2 Campbell, Monica, "Cuba's Book World, Above and Below Ground," *PRI's The World,* (July 2, 2012). https://www.pri.org/stories/2012—07—02/cubas—book—world—above—and—below—ground

3 Salinas, Marie Elena, "In Cuba, Books Can Lead to Prison Time," *Havana Journal* (April 25, 2004). http://havanajournal.com/politics/entry/in_cuba_books_can_lead_to_prison_time_opinion/

4 "Report on Cuban Issue," *American Library Association* (January 15, 2001). http://www.ala.org/aboutala/offices/iro/iroactivities/alacubanlibrariesreportcuban

A BOOK, A COLLECTION, OR A LIBRARY?

1 Hornby, Nick, *The Polysyllabic Spree* (San Francisco: Believer Books, 2004).

2 Spellings for Catherine of Aragon also appear as Katherine of Aragon equally.

3 Petroski, Henry, *The Book on the Book Shelf* (New York: Random House, 1999), 97.

4 Moorhouse, Geoffrey, *The Last Divine Office: Henry VIII and the Dissolution of Monasteries* (New York: Blue Bridge, 2012), 218.

5 Moorhouse, *The Last Divine Office,* 218.

BOOKS AS ART

1   The company received a patent in 2016 (United States Patent No. 9,349,308). The title of the patent and the summary is a bit jargon-y but the basic idea covered under the patent is this: How to print an image across multiple books.

DYNAMIC APPLICATION OF
A DESIGN ACROSS MULTIPLE
PRODUCT PACKAGES

Embodiments relate in general to image processing and more particularly, but not by way of limitation, to dynamic application of a display field design across a layout of multiple non-adjoined packaging surfaces.

2   Dickens, Charles, *Oliver Twist* (London: Penguin Classics, Reissue Edition, 2003).

BOOKS ABOUT YOUR HOBBIES AND INTERESTS

1   Murakami, Haruki, *Norwegian Wood* (New York: Vintage, 2000).

2   https://www.thedailymeal.com/cook/25-best-selling-cookbooks-all-time-slideshow/slide-3

BOOKS FOR CHILDREN

1   Hanushek, Eric A. and Ludger Woessmann, "The Economics of International Differences in Educational Achievement," http://ftp.iza.org/dp4925.pdf.

2   Prior, Karen Swallow, "How Reading Makes Us More Human," *Atlantic,* (June 21, 2013).

THE LIVING ROOM

1   Baldwin, Billy, quoted in: Stephens, Suzanne, "Cram Course: Living With Too Many Books," *New York Times* (September 5, 1985), section C1.

WHAT STAYS AND WHAT GOES

1   Miller, Henry, *The Books in My Life* (New York: New Directions, 1969).

2   Lloyd Alexander Interview Transcript. Scholastic. https://www.scholastic.com/teachers/articles/teaching—content/lloyd—alexander—interview—transcript/

READING THE BOOKS YOU HAVE

1   Blow, Charles, M. "Reading Books is Fundamental," *New York Times* (January 22, 2014).

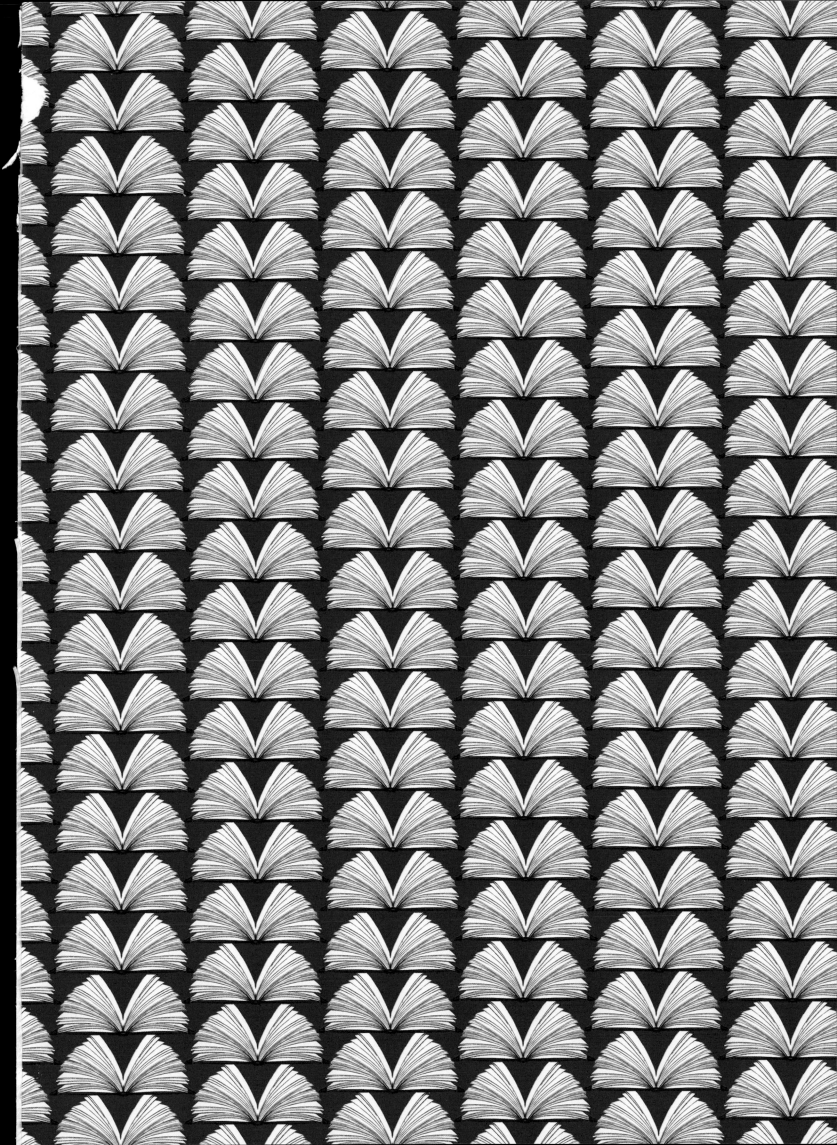

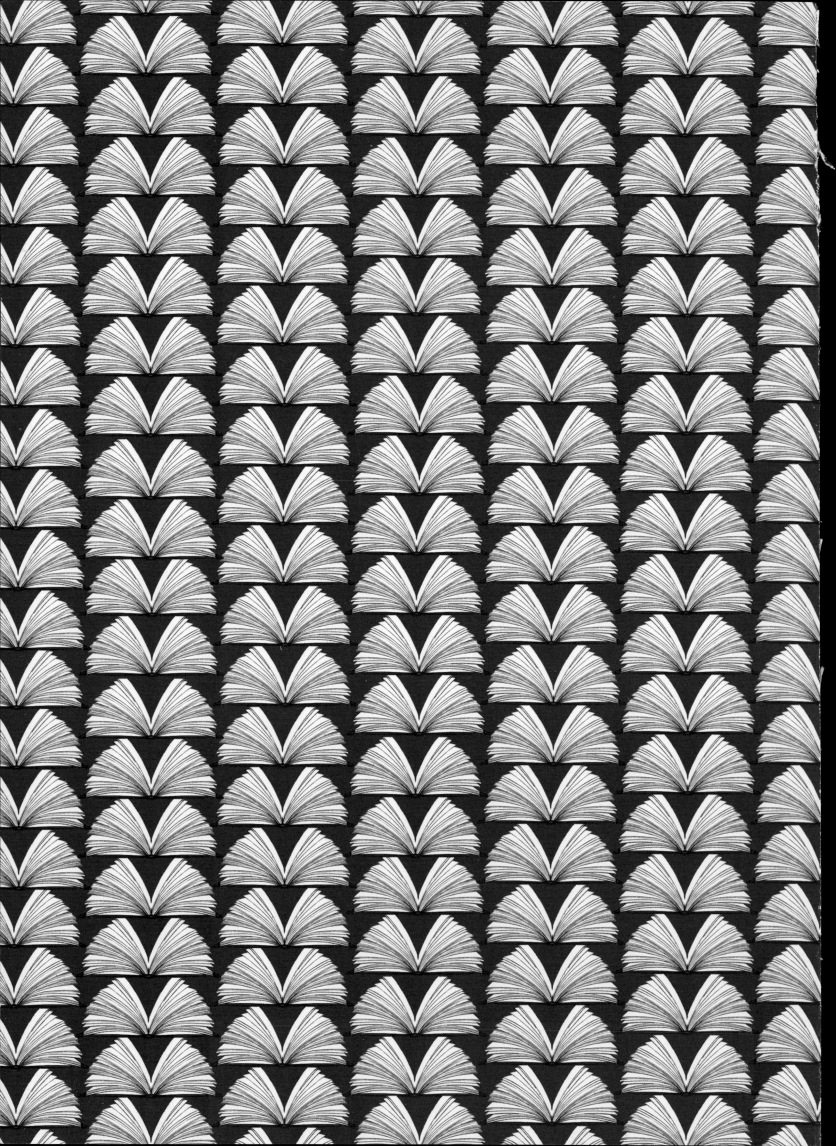